# Equity of Cybersecurity in the Education System

## High Schools, Undergraduate, Graduate and Post-Graduate Studies.

Equity in cybersecurity education for current and future high school, college, and university graduates serves as *a civilization of hope, the origin of a balanced vision, a matched promise and confidence in natural reliquary,* a guaranteed, and underpinning channel against perpetrators of cyber-crimes, cyber-threats, and cyber-attacks on global innocent vulnerable citizens in the free world and in the event of the next COVID-19 pandemic.

Joseph O. Esin

A Fellow at the Washington Center for Cybersecurity Research and Development

**author**HOUSE

*AuthorHouse™*
*1663 Liberty Drive*
*Bloomington, IN 47403*
*www.authorhouse.com*
*Phone: 833-262-8899*

*Published by AuthorHouse  03/23/2021*

*ISBN: 978-1-6655-2012-6 (sc)*
*ISBN: 978-1-6655-2011-9 (e)*

*Print information available on the last page.*

*This book is printed on acid-free paper.*

# Contents

# Acknowledgments

I am immensely grateful to my father, Worthy Maurice Akuda Okon Esin; my mother, Mrs. Felicia Nkoyo Eyo Esin; my paternal grandfather, Chief Esin Akuda Abasi; my paternal grandmother, Madam Afiong U. Abasi; my maternal grandfather, Chief Eyo A. Ulliong; and my maternal grandmother, Madam Iqwo A. Ekpa. I also would like to extend a special thank-you to Chief Clement E. Anthony, Professor Joseph A. Asor, Professor Emmanuel N. Ngwang, Professor Lester C. Newman, Professor Glenell Lee-Pruitt, Professor Benson Kariuki, Professor Tyson McMillan, Professor Jane LeClair, Dr. Lisa G. Lang, Dr. Felix M. Ekanem, John A. Ozo, Dr. Moses A. Agana, Joseph E. Ukpong, Prince O. Ana, Victor A. Rom, Victor B. Uno, Sunday B. Akan, Ekwere D. Ekwere, and Nicholas N. Edet for their sustained support and assistance. Special thanks are extended to all my family members, to Udung Esin, AFI-UDA, to the Uda group of villages, and to the Mbo and Oron communities for their unrelenting support.

# Introduction
## Distinguishing Guide

I must admit, cyberthreats, cyberattacks, and breaches of organizations' resources have outgrown every other risk factor faced by public and private organizations, institutions of higher education, and global security personnel. I unassertively appeal to academic professors, instructors, and educators to redouble their efforts with determination, commitment, and the willingness to accept the responsibility of establishing collaborative alliances with high schools, colleges, and universities to support, nurture, and promote equity of cybersecurity in education systems in different subject areas, including computer science, computer information systems, management information security, criminal justice, biology, and chemistry. The perils of cyberthreats, cyberattacks, unauthorized use, hacking and cracking, and data breaches are proliferating on every device connected to the internet and in every organization's secure storage center. Armed with ongoing indiscretion surrounding the use of the "true-to-life but frightful internet" for network connections, data storage, transmission, and communication in private and public organizations, higher education enterprises are strongly urged to restrain from adopting a lethargic byzantine approach to thwart collaborative efforts needed to battle existing looming threats of cybersecurity by advancing with aggressive steps and a well-structured plan of action to protect against, defend against, and eradicate the underlying forces of cybercrimes, cyberthreats, and cyberattacks against vulnerable, innocent citizens. Cybersecurity is an art of intellectual confrontation, utilizing the utmost in human intellectual ability in the battle zone, and it helps to place maximum responsibility on higher education administrators, professors, instructors, and educators for reorganizing most segments of their course offerings with singular, worldwide, user-friendly, unrestricted educational equipment to train the new generation. To gain expertise in cybercrimes, cyberthreats, cyberattacks, social engineering, and hacking is a long-term undertaking and requires continuing education from the fundamentals through graduate studies. Skill and expertise to battle cybersecurity threats must start by adopting equity in cybersecurity education as a fundamental point of reference, such as in high school through postgraduate programs.

Most professor, instructors, and educators graduated prior to the emergence of internet mayhem and cybersecurity, and prior to the era of course learning outcomes (CLO) and student learning outcomes (SLO). Components of student learning outcomes must include evidence-based practices of instruction style, methodology, and the use of assessment information, organized to meet the needs of students, satisfy the expectations of course offerings, meet program goals, provide measurable assessment tools, give feedback relative to academic performance and teaching effectiveness, and create an institutional mission, purpose, and philosophy. Cybersecurity is a challenging discipline involving rigorous algorithms; hence, course learning outcomes must each involve a self-justifying mechanism aiming at reinforcing professors' and educators' agreement to accept students into the academic program, ready and prepared to stimulate positive interactions in and out of the classroom, provide constructive and passive feedback, encourage teamwork among students, and implement different techniques to encourage active learning endeavors so students may become self-directed and independent critical thinkers.

Equity in cybersecurity education must be organized to provide an instructional, step-by-step approach to empower professors, instructors, and learners to face this swiftly growing threat to innocent citizens. Perpetrators of cyberattacks have expanded their sophisticated strategies to include various facilities, hacking and cracking into private and public financial data and other information using cyberwarfare, ransomware, and malware to intimidate and sabotage the landscape of the global community. Our private and public transmission and communication systems are unrestricted and without boundaries; the integration of mobile technology and electronic communication has increased, serving as host to more cyberattacks and cybercrimes, the perpetrators of which are sophisticated, organized, and often fully aware of the facilities they intend to target.

Amid the COVID-19 pandemic, the only unchallenged, obvious, all-inclusive concern is the health-care security of vulnerable private citizens. Notwithstanding world citizens' privacy, medical doctors, allied health-care professionals, national leaders, state governors, mayors, and local government representatives have emerged as the most effective, efficient, dependable, defensive, and offensive leaders in the battle against this world pandemic, a shattering episode. However, the pandemic seems to be girded by scriptural and mystical realities, as seen when analyzed mathematically; the COVID-19 pandemic (C = 100, 0 =79, V = 5, 1 = 1, D = 500; add these figures together to get 685. Subtract 19 from 685, and you get 666 [Revelation 13:18]) has brought the entire global community into challenging times marked by uncertain disorders amid intriguing questions that cause superpowers, middle powers, lower powers, and zero powers—First World, Second World, Third World, Fourth World, and Zero World nations—to remain humble and unassuming, untiringly acknowledging the glory of God's creation. God pronounced his glory, his wonders, and his blessings upon the worldly kingdom that he created (Job 38:18). God did not declare his servant Job innocent or guilty; hence, amid the COVID-19 pandemic, we must continue to work together, pray together, and refrain from declaring all God's dedicated and consecrated families on earth innocent or guilty.

Nations that are firmly engrained with stockpiles of nuclear weapons, with long-range, short-range, and no-range ballistic missiles that act like labor-saving-mechanical appliances such as washing machines, toasters, and photocopy machines, contain push buttons which give these leaders the unique and unprecedented opportunity to push just a button and have the inflict great devastation upon vulnerable innocent global citizens. Leaders with nuclear weapons seem determined to do everything humanly possible to destroy entire nations or regions that attempt to acquire nuclear weapons. Where are the nuclear missile buttons now that the COVID-19 pandemic is ringing the doorbell? COVID-19 operates on an exclusive agenda, one that cannot be changed or rescheduled, and in aberration of the new world order, demanding total obedience and submission to God's last pronouncement across the globe. In compliance with the new world order, global communities, including villages, cities, counties, local regions, states, and national organizations, are urged to assume equal responsibility for the reorganization and restructuring of functional rehabilitation by approving matching budgets for establishing well-suited pandemic hospitals, health-care facilities with well-matched medical equipment and supplies, and educational systems with well-suited instructional equipment and learning tools that are parallel to national military weapons budgets.

In light of President John F. Kennedy's assertion that you should ask what you can do for your country, not what your country can do for you, today, the

COVID-19 pandemic is ringing each nation's doorbell. World leaders are charged with doing what they can do for their countries, that is, to become effective, efficient, dependable, defensive, and offensive commanding officers who place their priority on a substantive increase in the budgets for education, health care, and the military. Amid the COVID-19 pandemic, the only unchallenged and all-inclusive concerns are the global health-care security of vulnerable private citizens and the fact that education systems all over the world have been closed with the learning process obstructed. I must admit, the health-care professionals and other frontline responders we have seen rise to the challenge during the COVID-19 pandemic are unquestionably the direct products of an educational system. The global priority is to increase budgets for education systems. This is the key to battling global cybersecurity threats and disease pandemics. Given the emerging open-ended anytime-and-anywhere cyberattacks and cybercrimes, along with the Ebola and COVID-19 pandemics, it is now imperative for citizens of the world community to become deeply involve in protecting and securing their nations.

# Author's Commitment

I am totally committed to listening and paying close attention to adopters, professors, instructors, educators, information technology (IT) administrators, forensic investigators, network security consultants, and readers who have chosen *Equity of Cybersecurity in the Education System* for high schools and institutions offering undergraduate, graduate, and postgraduate studies. International communities have intensified their dependency on cybersecurity operatives as a benchmark to battling global cybercrimes, cyberattacks, and breaches against private and public organizations, institutions of higher learning, and health-care establishments. Equity in cybersecurity education is a unifying academic force and a guaranteed benchmark calling on college and university settings—a fertile domain—and advocates of career professionals to reexamine current course offerings and adopt equity in cybersecurity education as a promising starting point for a successful future of resolving and mitigating cyberthreats and cyberattacks upon vulnerable, innocent citizens. Cybersecurity education is challenging by nature, including the instructional approach and methodologies, course learning outcomes (CLO), student learning outcomes (SLO), professional certifications, graduation rates, and employment. Notably, there is a massive group of dedicated and committed professors, instructors, and other educators who are willing and ready at all times to conquer cyberthreats, cyberattacks, and cybercrimes and to modify instructional pedagogies with a marching goal of successfully integrating cybersecurity degree programs to empower current and future generations with knowledge-based expertise so they may emerge as first responders in the battle against the fast-spreading cyberpandemic.

In light of the thought-provoking philosophy of cybersecurity operatives, professors, instructors, and other educators are urged to adopt ongoing instructional measurable assessments at the end of every four-month session; provide formative and summative reactions on the course learning outcomes (CLO); and acknowledge strengths, reflect growths and weaknesses, and highlight areas for further improvement. Positive responses and productive criticism is the natural podium for the restructuring of course offerings to create optimum instruction and learning expertise. Equity in cybersecurity education is not food for the hungry but is a progressive instructional approach involving face-to-face class meetings, research and discovery sessions, and virtual and online meetings where active participation is encouraged and cogent input is often greatly appreciated.

# Intended Audience

*Equity of Cybersecurity in the Education System* devotes chapters to course offerings, listed by subject area, for high schools; undergraduate, graduate, and postgraduates' studies; and professional certifications. The topics covered in each chapter as enumerated throughout the text include cybercrime, cyberthreats, and cyberattacks. Over the past twenty-five years, cybersecurity has evolved from an opaque discipline often enthroned in restricted facilities such as government agencies, financial institutions, and military operations. Today, cybersecurity crusades constitute the mainstream operations in most private and public organizations and institutions of higher education across the globe. Leading contributing factors to organizations, nations, and far-flung international cybersecurity operatives are the unrestricted growth of the internet, omnipresent connectivity, around-the-clock migration of vital data, other information, and intellectual property into a digital format, and the rapid outsourcing of critical data and information to cloud providers.

The emergence of cybersecurity amid a culture of parallel cybercriminal activity has translated to a huge demand for skilled, experienced, trained cybersecurity professionals who can engage in an all-out battle to decrease the terrifying and mutating threats of cybersecurity across the globe. I must admit that the world community, private and public organizations, systems of higher education, and the health-care industry need cybersecurity professionals with real-world experience. *Equity of Cybersecurity in the Education System* discusses practical application of cybersecurity within computer information systems to protect against cyberbarriers and protractors. Colleagues of the same school of thought support the assertion that every day and at any moment, cybercrime and cyberattack threats are inevitable and must be confronted as a global danger against human civilization. Because of the unpredictable nature of cyberattacks and cyberthreats, the battle must begin by ensuring equity of cybersecurity in education, along with the dedication and commitment to review course offerings in high schools and in undergraduate, graduate, and postgraduate institutions across the globe. *Equity of Cybersecurity in the Education System* is written to provide a sturdy foundation to protect private and public organizations, institutions of higher education, and the health-care sector against these inescapable cyberattacks and cyberthreats and also to provide an active plan of action to mitigate this all-inclusive, complex, and challenging anticipated threat to global security.

# Preamble

Equity of cybersecurity in education, beginning in high school and continuing in undergraduate, graduate, and postgraduate education, is a promising pathway to enhancing the integration of effective and efficient cybersecurity education curricula with an emphasis on collaboration to offer undergraduate, graduate, postgraduate, and professional certifications and expertise in cybersecurity to combat the ongoing criminal activity against vulnerable citizens. Most institutions in the United States, Europe, Africa, and Asia already offer undergraduate, graduate, and postgraduate degree programs and professional certifications in cybersecurity. The alarming rate of proliferation of such innovative methodologies serves as a forerunner, a groundbreaking effort, to bridge the gap and reduce the shortage of talented cybersecurity professionals in an attempt to uproot and eradicate the hazard of cyberthreats and cyberattacks on innocent vulnerable citizens. Equity in teaching cybersecurity skills and expertise must be supported by a well-structured and thought-out collaborative initiative involving a broad-ranging audience such as university and college professors, instructors and other educators, presidents of academic institutions, and leaders of organizations.

# Equity of Cybersecurity in Education

The era of instructional process and learning endeavors is a challenging one; hence, professors and educators must step forward, prepared and ready to transform methods of managing and delivering instruction accordingly. Converting the instruction and learning vehicle is a prerequisite to inspiring professors' and other educators' physical appearance at all class sessions, including instructional video displays and hands-on exercises, in furtherance of the aims of a well-thought-out syllabus enumerating course learning outcomes and student learning outcomes. A projected measurable learning approach requires that the course syllabus include pre-assessment measuring tools related to a career in cybersecurity. As I have written in an article, expertise, skills, and knowledge in the cybersecurity profession do not operate in a vacuum. Cybersecurity education, if it is to create people who have the ability to battle cyberthreats and cyberattacks, must be modulated according to the design and implementation process. Professors and educators are strongly urged to update and correlate their approach to equity in cybersecurity education given the frequency of security-related incidents, their practical impact, and the remedy to reduce the enormous impact of the damage created by lack of, or inadequacy of, a systematic approach.

Perpetrators of cyberthreats, cybercrimes, and cyberattacks, along with system hackers and crackers, are highly cognizant of existing social engineering activities. Equity in cybersecurity education is designed to mitigate perfunctory episodic and inadequate so-called training as an adequate pathway to protect against and eliminate cyberthreats and cyberattacks. An effective and unconventional strategy to battle cyberthreats and cyberattacks is the implementation of equitable cybersecurity education in high school, college, and university settings. Most private and public organizations and systems of higher education existed prior to the emergence of cybersecurity operations. Grounded in a projection of global security, the current generation is today charged and empowered as active participants with the ability to use existing electronic tools and devices to battle cyberthreats, cybercrimes, cyberattacks, and data breaches. The unconcluded and unexpected battle against perpetrators of cyberthreats requires competencies derived from active education; expertise; skills; and the elimination of deception in cybersecurity education.

# Foundation of Cybersecurity

Cyberthreats and cyberattacks rank remarkably high as compared to every other risk against global security, public and private organizations, financial institutions, political parties, and critical infrastructure around the world. The perils of cyberthreats and cyberattacks are proliferating on every device connected to the internet that is neither safeguarded against by the manufacturer nor secured by the user. Armed with ongoing indiscretion surrounding the use of the "true to life but frightful internet" for data transmission and communication, private and public organizations and the entire enterprise of higher education are strongly urged to restrain from taking the prevalent lethargic byzantine approach that is currently in motion to thwart the collaborative effort needed to mitigate existing looming threats to cybersecurity and step forward with a structured plan of action to protect and defend against cyberthreats and cyberattacks.

Nations, states, counties, local governments, cities, and villages are derivatives of a singular population originating from babies in diapers to adults in suits, a populace considered to be highly receptive and relaxed, a repository for breathing and sentience. History shows that there is an established culture of high school educators, college and university professors, instructors, and higher education administrators. State and federal education systems are urged to intensify their support for promoting cybersecurity education as a universal point of reference to mitigate human error in attempts to battle cybercrimes, cyberthreats, and cyberattacks. Cybersecurity arose in the era of mainframe computers, which had the minutest levels of security to protect the growing needs of a vulnerable community or to battle against the most sophisticated perpetrators of cyberattacks. Cybercrimes, cyberthreats, and cyberattacks were in existence, but they were not as volatile or explosive as those of our generation. The underlying theory behind cyberthreats and cyberattacks calls for the urgent need to educate and prepare doyens and professionals so they may decrease the great number of cyberthreats and cyberattacks using all-inclusive measures.

# Academic Professors', Instructors', and Educators' Operatives

◇◇◇◇◇◇◇◇◇◇◇◇◇◇◇◇◇◇◇◇◇◇◇◇◇◇◇◇◇◇◇◇◇◇◇◇◇◇◇◇◇◇◇◇◇◇◇◇◇◇◇◇◇◇

As I wrote in my article "Eliminating Gender Disparity in Cybersecurity Professions through Education," published in 2018, the implementation of cybersecurity education will certainly decrease, thereby escalating the cyberthreats and cyberattacks perpetrated against the current and future generations who intend to reside in states and nations where job opportunities are promising with reachable career goals, along with respect and dignity afforded upon completion of a rigorous academic cybersecurity program.

As I wrote in my 2018 article, most professors, educators, staff, and students are unaware of measures put in place to prevent risky behaviors leading to a security breach against an organization's data and other information in the era of BYOD (bring your own device) and social media. The best security and the best protective measure against cyberattacks is to create a professional alliance and engage in constructive, tailored education in cybersecurity as an acceptable guideline for high school educators and college and university professors for managing and delivering instruction and for learning endeavors that are serviceable in cyberoperations. This is in no way an attempt to turn academic professors, high school educators, and other personnel into global bodyguards, but it is an attempt to solve a problem that is on the rise through learning about cybersecurity and then securing, managing, controlling, and protecting clients' data and other information and preventing the illegal sharing of data on social media sites. Stimulating partnerships and collaborative cybersecurity education programs in high schools and in undergraduate, graduate, and postgraduate programs will positively empower the current generation and future generations with the skills, expertise, and tenacity needed to battle cyberattacks and will guarantee and reinforce the growth of job opportunities in cybersecurity across the globe. A projected cybersecurity education program must be designed to inspire hope, temper public fear, and eradicate the proliferation of cyberattacks, cyberthreats, cybercrime, and cyberterrorism against vulnerable and innocent citizens.

The traditional template for the integration of an equitable cybersecurity education program into existing degree programs must begin by offering five courses in which students prepare to earn industry certification and accumulate credit hours that are transferred to and accepted by a Bachelor of Science degree program offered by a regional accredited institution. The template of five required courses includes an introduction to cybersecurity, principles of networking security, wireless and mobile networking, defensive and offensive ethical hacking, and defensive security.

# Equity in Cybersecurity
# Education Algorithm

◇◇◇◇◇◇◇◇◇◇◇◇◇◇◇◇◇◇◇◇◇◇◇◇◇◇◇◇◇◇◇◇◇◇◇◇◇◇◇◇◇◇◇◇◇◇◇◇◇◇◇◇◇◇◇◇◇◇◇◇◇

High schools, colleges, and universities admit candidates into the educational system, whereas professors and educators are responsible for accept candidates into a degree program. Admission indicates the strength, quality, determination, citizenship, and potential to belong to the educational community of a candidate. Acceptance often reinforces strength, appreciation, kindness, and sharing, which equips the candidate to successfully complete the degree program. Professors and educators, your acceptance constitutes an acknowledgment of the academic agreement to provide quality instruction and accommodations so that candidates may endurance and go on to successfully complete the degree program. Faculty and educators must be willing to redouble their efforts to advise students on the consequences of not completing a college degree. In Africa, parents toil and sweat to pay for their children's education from grade school through undergraduate and graduate school, and recipients of such education are often saddled with personal shame and family humiliation. In the United States, parents sacrifice their hard-earned income to pay for their children's education, along with using financial aid and loans, and the recipients of such education are challenged with the personal and filial indignity of paying the money back to the federal or state government regardless.

The education process is an open-ended and enduring continuum to provide everybody a chance to fulfill their educational potential and bring their potential to fruition at any time in life, thereby allowing them to reconnect with and recapture missed opportunities regardless of age, gender, nationality, creed, or religion. The author professes that collaborative endeavors with regard to all components of an education in cybersecurity should extend beyond completion of the loop to focus on the mission of battling against perpetrators of cyberattacks and cyberthreats committed against a vulnerable and innocent global society. This salient point rests on professors' and other educators' willingness to step away from the bureaucracy's overwhelming agenda and to meet students during class sessions, or in the hallway, library, or cafeteria, to shake hands and ask simple questions such as "How are you? What is your name? What is your major? How are your studies going?" The believable by-product of lifelong education is the restoration of hope, along with a sense of personal and professional fulfillment in the minds of enrolled learners, institutions, family, and the community. I am convinced that no knowledge is a waste; hence, a lasting education lays a concrete foundation to lead current and future generations toward a culture with resourceful, healthy, civilized people and an acceptable standard of living. Education is the foundation of wisdom, enhancement of high-quality and ethical judgments, spiritual growth, economic advancement, personal growth, professional development, and societal freedom.

I must admit, cyberthreats and cyberattacks have outgrown every other risk there is against global security, public and private organizations, and institutions of higher education. I unassumingly appeal to all academic professors and other educators to redouble their efforts with determined commitment and a willingness to accept the responsibility of establishing collaborative alliances with high schools, colleges, and universities to support, nurture, and promote cybersecurity endeavors. Given the vigor of cyberthreats and cyberattacks, higher-education administrators, academic professors, and other educators are required to establish comprehensive educational standards, codes of conduct, policies, and procedures to advance learning endeavors and retain qualified academicians who are imbued with the ability to handle internal and external academic undertakings, including students' emotional welfare, to battle cyberthreats and cyberattacks.

# Culture of Instructional Delivery

◇◇◇◇◇◇◇◇◇◇◇◇◇◇◇◇◇◇◇◇◇◇◇◇◇◇◇◇◇◇◇◇◇◇◇◇◇◇◇◇◇◇◇◇◇◇◇◇◇◇◇◇◇◇◇◇◇◇◇◇◇◇◇◇◇◇◇◇◇

Cybersecurity is a fast-growing field involving the use technologies and acquired professional expertise to protect the electronic data, information, resources, and assets of public and private organizations and institutions of higher education from perpetrators. Professors, instructors, and other educators must give precedence to subject areas of the cybersecurity platform to ensure that the academic program meets the course learning outcomes and student learning outcomes. Individual and group student projects must be structured in such a way to empower and promote understanding of skills, knowledge-based communication, and social skills; teach how to work interdependently; and reinforce self-efficacy. Cybersecurity is an innovative algorithm demanding reinforcement, constructive feedback, a display of cultural sensitivity, and open communication and must be empirically supported in an attempt to liberate and empower high school students to pursue a lifetime career in this field, as such individuals are much needed across the globe. Equity in cybersecurity education instruction and learning must emphasize quality over quantity, and real-world application over opinion. Real-world application and quality instruction and learning often allows students to achieve mastery when it comes to understanding how to battle the cyberthreats and cyberattacks that are tearing the world community into pieces.

Cybersecurity is a guaranteed benchmark for data and information transmission and communication in a global digital community. A collaborative cybersecurity curriculum from high school to college is a stand-alone accelerated road map to mitigate every minute and everyday cybersecurity threat. There is virtually zero unemployment among cybersecurity professionals, and the global demand will soon outpace the supply of cybersecurity professionals at every level in the next fifteen years. As I discuss in my aforementioned article published in 2017, equity in cybersecurity education unifies the academic force and is a guaranteed benchmark. Here and now, I am calling on college and university settings that

8

are fertile domains for and advocates of practical employment to reexamine their current academic curriculums and include collaborative cybersecurity education so as to guide students to protect against a possible cyberattack of historic scale against the global community. Education will never go out of business or expire. It is a promising landscape for the future goal of resolving and mitigating against the cyberthreats and cyberattacks committed against vulnerable innocent citizens. Cyberthreats, immeasurable by nature, call for an all-hands-on-deck approach beginning in high school and spanning across colleges and university education. At this time, an all-hands-on-deck approach is needed in the battle against global cybersecurity threats as perpetrators are becoming progressively more sophisticated, but the collective global village has the resources and manpower to deploy in this war in order to succeed. All it requires is good faith and a collective endeavor and trust among academic professors, instructors, and other educators.

Consider the incident on September 5, 2019, at the College of Central Florida (CCF), where a hacker knew that President James Henningsen was out of town according to Henry Glaspie, associate vice president for information technology. The perpetrator, posing as the president, sent an email to another vice president confirming that his credit card had been stolen and saying he needed someone to wire money to him. Although this email was not sent directly to a student, still, students need to be educated on how to battle cyberthreats physically, emotionally, and psychologically. Some college and university students are enrolled in the Army Reserve Officers' Training Corps (ROTC), an educational program that combines college electives in military science with practical and unmatched leadership skills. The sets of courses offered by high schools, colleges, and universities must be reexamined, and courses should be added to allow students the opportunity to become leaders in the field of cybersecurity by pairing with people of unmatched leadership in cybersecurity internships with the United States Department of Homeland Security and the United States Department of the Navy.

The best security and the best protective measure against cyberthreats and cyberattacks is to create a professional alliance as a guideline for high school educators and college professors in the managing and delivery of instruction and learning endeavors. Cybersecurity, like other academic disciplines, is a challenging, rigorous, and time-consuming program, requiring an intellectual approach through partnerships and alliances with professional organizations. The new generation, from the high school level to the college and university level, is a credible instrument to foster intrinsic motivation, but it requires a precise length of time for training, understanding, and adjustment. Therefore, an equally high degree of dedication and commitment is required of the students, high school educators, college and university professors, and parents. The education system is a universal promising center intended to develop solutions to eradicate cyberattacks against innocent global citizens.

The establishment of a professional career advisory board (PCAB) is crucial. Projected members of the PCAB must include high school educators, college and university professors, parents, a US Navy representative from the Cybersecurity Unit, a representative from the Department of Homeland Security, and elected student representatives.

The lifelong answer to battling the global scourge of cyberthreats is to heighten understanding, reinforce integrated course offerings, and provide a practical and unmatched professional education to eradicate cyberattacks against vulnerable innocent citizens. Higher-education administrators often ignore cyberthreats and fail to incorporate funding for cyberthreats into the organization's annual budget. Cyberthreats are a credible imminent danger worldwide, requiring an intellectual approach through partnerships and alliances with high school educators, college and university professors, a representative from the navy's Cybersecurity Unit, parents, and a representative from Homeland Security.

Professors, instructors, and educators are urged to engage in activity-based self-regulated skills, self-direction, self-awareness, learning strategies, and empowerment to improve their personal and professional lives. An emphasis on measurable outcomes—course learning outcomes (CLO) and student learning outcomes (SLO)—in cybersecurity course offerings, and on acquired expertise and discipline in the degree program, is important as these are the things students need to know.

# Philosophy of Student Learning Outcomes

Most professors and educators graduated prior to the era of the internet and cybersecurity, course learning outcomes, and student learning outcomes. Components of student learning outcomes (SLO) must include evidence-based practices of instructional style, methodology, and the use of assessment information, organized to meet the needs of students, including their expectations of the course offerings, and to further program goals; conduct assessments; provide feedback relative to academic performance and teaching effectiveness; and further the institution's mission, purpose, and philosophy. Student learning outcomes must include an evaluation of instructional approach and methodology in most subject areas beginning in high school and continuing on into undergraduate, graduate, and postgraduate studies. SLO has emerged as a major focus of concern relative to instruction and learning across the United States' education systems and as comfort zones for professors and educators to interact, leading to an expansion of a successful academic future and the acquisition of leadership skills (Esin 2016; Allison 2015; Komarraju, Musulkin, and Bhattacharya 2010).

The sudden increase of cybersecurity has exerted extensive influence on the system of higher education. Prior to the emergence of cyberattacks and cyberthreats, the education system was deficient in systematic uniform measures to prepare current and future generations for the intellectual battle, not for physical artillery and assault weapon combat (Hammer, Piascik, Medina, Pettinger, Rose, Creekmore, Soltis, Bouldin, Schwarz, and Scott 2010). Cybersecurity is the art of intellectual confrontation utilizing the utmost in human intellectual ability in the battle zone. Cybersecurity has placed maximum responsibility on higher education administrators, professors, and other educators. Course offerings across the globe are being fully restructured toward a common goal, with a singular worldwide user-friendly and unrestricted weapon for training an expert territorial army to defend such a thing as the internet. Who would have thought the internet would become a platform for natural global disaster for a person of any generation on earth. Today, the area of higher education is the combat zone for cybersecurity operations. Current and future generations must be suitably equipped with the skills and expertise needed to fight this open-ended battle against vulnerable innocents. The development of expertise in cybercrimes, cyberthreats, cyberattacks, social engineering, and hacking is long term and requires continuing education from the fundamentals through graduate studies. Skill and expertise to battle cybersecurity threats must be rooted in the rudiments learned in high school and must be developed through postgraduate programs. Institutions should adopt cybersecurity education as an acceptable point of reference.

# Significance of Course Learning Outcomes

◇◇◇◇◇◇◇◇◇◇◇◇◇◇◇◇◇◇◇◇◇◇◇◇◇◇◇◇◇◇◇◇◇◇◇◇◇◇◇◇◇◇◇◇◇◇◇◇◇◇◇◇◇◇◇◇◇◇◇◇◇◇◇◇

The defense of cyberspace by means of a singular worldwide user-friendly, unrestricted weapon such as the internet by a trained expert group is a problem to which serious thought must be given. The purpose of equity in cybersecurity education is to eradicate the alarming number of cyberthreats and cyberattacks against vulnerable innocent citizens. The education setting is a dynamic and stable place to prepare both a defensive army and an offensive army against this expensive and explosive operation. Course learning outcomes (CLO) are a self-justifying mechanism reinforcing professors' and educators' agreement to accept students into the academic program. Professors and other educators must be thrilled, ready and prepared to stimulate positive interactions in and out of the classroom, provide constructive and passive feedback, encourage teamwork among students, have at their disposal different techniques to encourage active learning endeavors, thereby leading students to become self-directed, independent critical thinkers (Hammer, Piascik, Medina, Pettinger, Rose, Creekmore, Soltis, Bouldin, Schwarz, and Scott, 2010). An all-inclusive instructional process requires modification and mastery of the subject areas relative to defensive and offensive instruction. To secure further commitment validating the CLO agreement, professors and other educators are urged to remain culturally sensitive, courteous, and passionate, appealing to and challenging defensive and offensive cybersecurity leaders to reach their full potential while having reasonable expectations, participating in class, and demanding higher order thinking to stimulate discussions.

# Student Learning Outcomes in Cybersecurity Course Offerings

◇◇◇◇◇◇◇◇◇◇◇◇◇◇◇◇◇◇◇◇◇◇◇◇◇◇◇◇◇◇◇◇◇◇◇◇◇◇◇◇◇◇◇◇◇◇◇◇◇◇◇◇◇◇◇◇◇◇◇◇◇◇◇◇◇◇

Student learning outcomes (SLO) and course learning outcomes (CLO) are regulated by four components: professors, the educational system, cybersecurity aspirants, and vulnerable citizens. Three of these entities, professors, the education system, and cybersecurity aspirants, are obligated to be defenseless. Having spent thirty-two years in higher-education administration and instruction, I must admit that CLO and SLO cybersecurity education cannot operate in a vacuum. Professors and educators designated as the first responders in this global battle must be empowered with the tools and equipment to fully utilize their academic backgrounds, knowledge, and skills to amplify their intrinsic and extrinsic motivation to accommodate and mentor current and future cybersecurity professionals. Current cyberthreats and cyberattacks may be uncomfortable, but future cyberthreats and cyberattacks are unknown and are highly likely to be devastating and damaging. Take an approach to the instructional and learning process that includes auditory learning, visual learning, and essential supporting materials. Pedagogical competence ensures the combatant and society alike of a promising opportunity to complete a program with a concentration in cybersecurity, or an undergraduate or graduate degree in cybersecurity, and to gain the expertise needed to protect and defend the society.

# Structure of the Course Offerings

Unit 1  Origin of Cybersecurity
Unit 2  Eminence of Professors and Educators
Unit 3  Philosophy of Student Learning Outcomes (SLO)
Unit 4  Philosophy of Course Learning Outcomes (CLO)
Unit 5  Culture of SLO and CLO in Promoting Cybersecurity Education
Unit 6  Five Courses, High School Diploma through Undergraduate Degree
       Course Structure—High School (HS) and Bachelor of Science (BSc)
       HS-BD-1   Fundamentals of Cybersecurity
       HS-BD-2   Principles of Networking Security
       HS-BD-3   Wireless and Mobile Networking
       HS-BD-4   Defensive and Offensive Ethical Hacking
       HS-BD-5   Defensive Security
Unit 7  Bachelor of Science in Cybersecurity
Unit 8  Bachelor of Science Concentration
       Computer Science, Computer Information Systems, and Management
       Security
Unit 9  Master of Science (MSc) in Cybersecurity
Unit 10 Professional Certification, Practice Examination Banks

# Five Funneling Courses:
# High School through Postgraduate Studies

◇◇◇◇◇◇◇◇◇◇◇◇◇◇◇◇◇◇◇◇◇◇◇◇◇◇◇◇◇◇◇◇◇◇◇◇◇◇◇◇◇◇◇◇◇◇◇◇◇◇◇◇

Many members of the academic community often argue that high school education systems should be exempted from having to provide equitable cybersecurity education. I subscribe to the belief of one segment of the academic community permitting an equitable cybersecurity program in high schools, undergraduate institutions, and postgraduate programs. Cybersecurity threats, cyberattacks, identity theft, intellectual property theft, electronic fraud, and cyberterrorism can all be minimized through equitable cybersecurity education. Current and future cybergraduates would like to live in states and nations where there are promising job opportunities and reachable career goals, and where one is treated with respect and dignity upon completion of a rigorous cybersecurity academic program. Equitable cybersecurity education is not an attempt to turn current and future professors and educators into global bodyguards, but a natural and conscientious determined effort to protect and defend society against cyberattacks. Upon a student's successful completion of the program in high school, colleges and universities must be willing to serve as a nucleus to offer a similar program in multiple high schools, which I am sure will help to eradicate cybercrime, cyberthreats, and cyberattacks across the globe.

Acceptance of equity in cybersecurity education in high schools, undergraduate institutions, and postgraduate programs will empower the new generation with the skills, expertise, and tenacity to battle cybersecurity attacks, thereby guaranteeing a large number of job opportunities in cybersecurity across the globe. Course offerings must be designed in partnership with high schools, undergraduate, graduate, and postgraduate programs, and United States Cyber Command. To enhance successful operation of as cybersecurity education program, professors, instructors, and other educators are urged to form an education alliance, including a steering cybersecurity advisory board (SCAB). Members of the SCAB must include high school educators, students' parents, representatives of United States Cyber Command, and academic professors, instructors, and other educators. Education is an enduring conduit to acquiring knowledge, skills, expertise, sovereign reasoning, ethical and moral judgment, intelligence, maturity, and a lifelong profession. Operatives implementing measures to achieve equity in cybersecurity education must recognize the importance of the collegiate family unit and must view family as a divinely appointed institution guided by parents who are often sympathetic with victims of cybersecurity attacks. Such parents have the ability to influence their children to believe in and accept an education in the field of cybersecurity as a challenging and rewarding personal and professional option.

I am a theologian by profession, but twenty-five years ago, my body, mind, soul, and intellectual power were entrenched in intensive negotiations about switching from theology (arts) to computer information systems and cybersecurity (science), which was not a smooth-sailing journey. Turning from one's original career path in search of a new profession is an intended risk and equally a recovery opportunity to overcome surprising challenges and ensure a successful personal and professional future. Graduating high school seniors and college freshmen must be encouraged by professors, instructors, other educators, a steering cybersecurity advisory board, and parents to embrace equity of cybersecurity in education and accept the field as one providing long-term opportunities, thereby giving these students the ability to circumvent intimidation and uncertainty so that they may become active representatives of the cybersecurity profession.

The field of cybersecurity is growing at a rapid pace; job opportunities for aspirants in the field of cybersecurity are now stronger across the globe than ever before. A paradigm shift, reflected in the equitable offering of cybersecurity as a choice in education, from high school to postgraduate degree programs, has placed instantaneous pressure on the current generation, who are extremely defensive against and unreceptively aggressive toward innovative career strategy until what they are seeking becoming available and is imminent. Cybercriminals are working twenty-four hours a day, seven days a week, to create and re-create opportunities to launch cyberattacks. An education in cybersecurity, starting with the fundamentals and moves through to the expert level, is a universally promising solution for eradicating cyberattacks against innocent citizens worldwide. Many millennials' professors, instructors, and other educators have limited knowledge of an education in cybersecurity, having never taking cybersecurity courses in high school through to the postgraduate level.

The emphasis of *Equity of Cybersecurity in the Education System* is on the integration of five courses across the academic curriculum. Given the growing global demand for skilled and experienced cybersecurity professionals, a higher weight is being placed on higher education that is innovative, and institutions of higher education are being held accountable for the success of their cybersecurity graduates who are launched into careers battling the endemic problem of cybercrimes, cyberthreats, and cyberattacks against global citizens. Ensuring access to an education in cybersecurity will be a better horizon to look toward for private and public organizations, and federal and state governments, when they show a willingness to offer continuing assistance and support, increase education budgets, provide donations, and collaborate in partnership with professors, instructors, and other educators as these professional's endeavor to increase the pool of cybersecurity professionals across the globe. The most ardent and impassioned organizations on the planet are educational institutions, but they often operate with limited resources. An army brigade cannot win any war using guns empty of bullets. For too long, education systems have been beset by too many liabilities. Today, amid the COVID-19 pandemic, with digital, data, and information rifts being endemic, private and public organizations, and federal and state governments, must be willing and ready to accept responsibility by unreservedly pouring out support upon institutions of higher education in an all-out effort to battle the global online data / digital information epidemic. A mounting reliance on online digital transmission has turned out to reveal a disconcerting number of cyberthreats, cybercrimes, and cyberattacks on private businesses, public organizations, and institutions of higher education.

In the past, cybersecurity education was integrated with the engineering and computer science domain owing to an unsettling stream of cyberattacks and cyberthreats against defenseless citizens; this recommends that cybersecurity be integrated across a broad range of academic disciplines. Traditionally, most course offerings are multidepartment, reflecting the universal nature of cybercrime, cyberthreats, and cyberattacks, and the majority of higher-education institutions offer undergraduate, graduate, and postgraduate degree programs and professional certifications in support of an academic diploma. In the United States, the Army Reserve Officers' Training Corps (ROTC) is an educational program that combines high school courses and college credit courses, as electives, with practical unmatched leadership. As a matter of urgency, education systems must reexamine their high school, undergraduate, and graduate programs' course offerings and encourage their cybersecurity students, with the help of cybersecurity professors and other educators, to apply for cybersecurity internships with the United States Army, the United States Navy, and the United States Department of Homeland Security's Cybersecurity Unit. Equity in cybersecurity education is a promising conduit for a successful future, aiming at resolving and mitigating global cybersecurity risks and attacks. In the present day, with the paradox of the borderless nature of digital data and information breaches, the author calls for an all-hands-on-deck approach, which begins with awareness to promote and support the field of cybersecurity in education. It is a difficult battle because perpetrators of cybercrime are seemingly increasingly sophisticated, but collectively, with available resources and deployment of skills and experienced manpower, we will succeed in defeating them.

To achieve equity with regard to an education in cybersecurity, from high school through postgraduate studies, requires credible, rigorous, proactive measures to place pressure on the current generation of students, who are extremely defensive, unreceptive, and aggressive toward innovative career strategy until such strategy becomes available and is imminent. The five-course structure, from high school (HS) to Bachelor of Science (BSc) degree, is designed to support a culture of equity in cybersecurity education. The five courses must be a part of the institution's approved course offerings leading to an undergraduate degree in cybersecurity, and only graduating twelfth grade students with an interest in cybersecurity, computer science, management information security, forensic chemistry, or biology should be allowed to register for the courses since all credits earned in the five courses are inclusive in the degree plan. The support in the battle against cybercrimes, cyberthreats, cyberattacks, and digital data breaches is further amplified by holding most of these class sessions on high school campuses based on the population of the registered students.

HS-BD-1  Fundamentals of Cybersecurity
HS-BD-2  Principles of Networking Security
HS-BD-3  Wireless and Mobile Networking
HS-BD-4  Defensive and Offensive Ethical Hacking
HS-BD-5  Defensive Security

# Course Descriptions: Five Funneling Courses with Related CLO and SLO

◇◇◇◇◇◇◇◇◇◇◇◇◇◇◇◇◇◇◇◇◇◇◇◇◇◇◇◇◇◇◇◇◇◇◇◇◇◇◇◇◇◇◇◇◇◇◇◇◇◇◇◇

## 1. HS-BS-1 Fundamentals of Cybersecurity

### Course Description

Fundamentals of Cybersecurity provides an introductory study of cybersecurity terminology, principles, and technologies. Fundamental topics covered include cyberthreats and vulnerabilities, information security frameworks, network infrastructure security, wireless network security, cryptography, defense-in-depth security strategy, information security policy, and security management. The goal is to develop a foundation for further study in cybersecurity (3 credit hours).

### Course Learning Outcomes (CLO)

Fundamental concepts of cyberdefense, identification of cyberdefense tools, methodology, security mechanisms, technical and personnel-driven cyberthreats, symmetric and asymmetric algorithms used in encryption schemas, and implementation of secure architecture and infrastructures.

### Student Learning Outcomes (SLO)

Upon completing this course, students will have acquired the expertise to examine and identify threat agents and bad actors to networks, including those involved in cyberterrorism and industrial espionage; analyze defense-in-depth as it relates to layers of the OSI model; interpret cyberdefense concepts to determine practical implementation methods; formulate and hypothesize how to implement tools and methods in defense of an attack; analyze system compromise activities and mitigations; scrutinize the first principles of network security, including security risk assessment; compare security mechanisms and determine how to implement them in a network; compare and contrast symmetric and asymmetric algorithms used in encryption schemas; analyze technologies and components used to defend networks against security issues to determine priority order in placement; and implement and utilize network monitoring tools.

## 2. HS-BS-2 Principles of Networking Security I

### Course Description

This course provides students with essential knowledge and techniques for securely installing, configuring, maintaining, and troubleshooting a computer network. Students first become familiar with the basics of networking. With the fundamentals in place, the course moves on to cover installing interface cards, managing static and dynamic IP addressing, setting up a wired or wireless network, configuring network security, managing network traffic, and configuring remote access to a network. Students learn how to maintain network security throughout these processes (3 credit hours).

### Course Learning Outcomes (CLO)

Networking basics, cables and connections, networking devices, Ethernet, IP configuration, switch management, routing, firewalls, network customization, wireless networking, wide area networks (WANs), network policies and procedures, network security, network hardening, network management, and network optimization.

### Student Learning Outcomes (SLO)

Upon completion of the course, students will have comprehensive knowledge of basic networking concepts such as network topologies, the Open Systems Interconnection model (OSI model), network protocols, cables and connectors, network devices, and Ethernet architecture. Students will examine IP addressing and IP services such as Dynamic Host Configuration Protocol (DHCP) and the domain name system (DNS); apply basic management of routing and switching; configure firewalls and customize networks; set up wired and wireless networks; implement elements of network security; apply network management concepts; and implement network optimization concepts.

## 3. HS-BS-3 Wireless and Mobile Networking

### Course Description

The course will provide students with in-depth knowledge of technologies used to implement wireless and mobile networks in a secure manner. Topics covered include wireless network components; types of wireless networks; network protocols; network performance and management; mobile systems and devices; nomenclature and implementation of mobile computing; mobile operating systems; cellular 3G, 4G, LTE, and 5G networks; and mobile device management. The course also assesses security risks to mobile and wireless technologies and explores the application of appropriate security controls (3 credit hours).

### Course Learning Outcomes (CLO)

Modern wireless and mobile networks; long-term evolution (4G LTE); 5G; small cells, security, and privacy; WPAN, WLAN, and Wi-Fi; WiMAX and WRAN; Internet of Things architecture and security; SS7/C7, signaling, and security; and wireless and mobile security.

### Student Learning Outcomes (SLO)

Upon completion of the course, students will be able to compare and contrast various mobile networks; examine the use of long-term evolution (LTE) architecture in system evolution, network discovery, and security; analyze advanced mobile architecture such as 5G and small cells; investigate wireless networks from close-distance to wide-area regional networks; analyze Internet of Things (IoT) networks, radio frequency identification (RFID), and near-field communication (NFC); and evaluate cloud, network virtualization, and wireless security.

## 4. HS-BS-4 Defensive and Offensive Ethical Hacking

### Course Description

The course is designed to provide students with an understanding of the approach hackers take in compromising a system. This approach is the same for criminal hackers as it is for ethical hackers, also known as penetration testers. The course examines hacking tools and techniques used by security professionals and ethical hackers to protect an organization's systems and data. It includes topics such as attack vectors, honeypots, penetration testing, and security baseline analyzers.

### Course Learning Outcomes (CLO)

An introduction to all types of defensive and offensive hackers, ethical hacking concepts, the ordered steps and phases in a hack, specific tools that can be used in each phase of an attack, social engineering, active and passive techniques, sniffing, scanning, gaining access, and hiding evidence.

### Student Learning Outcomes (SLO)

Upon completion of the course, students will be able to process the activities related to each hacking phase; employ hacking tools to conduct reconnaissance; investigate the security posture of system using ethical hacking; compare and contrast the types of hackers; and determine the appropriate tools to use in the appropriate phases.

## 5. HS-BS-5 Defensive Security

### Course Description

The course is designed to prepare students for securing networks from the network administrator's perspective with an emphasis on network security, data and host security, compliance and operation security, access control, identity management, and cryptography. Students will assess cybersecurity risks to networks, evaluate and select appropriate technologies, and apply prevention and detection strategies to defend networks (3 credit hours).

### Course Learning Outcomes (CLO)

Information, cybersecurity, and physical basics; policies and procedures; perimeter defense; network defense; application security; and data defense.

### Student Learning Outcomes (SLO)

Upon completion of the course, students will have acquired the ability to assess basic security measures to the enterprise; explore cybersecurity policies, procedures, and appropriate risk mitigation strategies; apply physical defensive measures for the organization's environment; examine perimeter attacks and appropriate defenses; apply security measures to network hardware; apply various methods to harden hosts and the operating systems; assess networking tools and protocols for access control, authentication, authorization, and other user activities; and evaluate the effectiveness of different encryption methodologies and the best practices of data management.

# Course Offerings:
# Bachelor of Science in Cybersecurity

◇◇◇◇◇◇◇◇◇◇◇◇◇◇◇◇◇◇◇◇◇◇◇◇◇◇◇◇◇◇◇◇◇◇◇◇◇◇◇◇◇◇◇◇◇◇◇◇◇◇◇◇◇

## 1. BS-1 Fundamentals of Cybersecurity

### Course Description

Fundamentals of Cybersecurity provides an introductory study of cybersecurity terminology, principles, and technologies. Fundamental topics covered include cyberthreats and vulnerabilities, information security frameworks, network infrastructure security, wireless network security, cryptography, defense-in-depth security strategy, information security policy, and security management. The goal is to develop a foundation for further study in cybersecurity (3 semester hours).

### Course Learning Outcomes (CLO)

Fundamental concepts of cyberdefense, identification of cyberdefense tools, methodology, security mechanisms, technical and personnel-driven cyberthreats, symmetric and asymmetric algorithms used in encryption schemas, and implementation of secure architecture and infrastructures.

### Student Learning Outcomes (SLO)

Upon completing this course, students will have acquired the expertise to examine and identify threat agents and bad actors to networks, including those involved in cyberterrorism and industrial espionage; analyze defense-in-depth as it relates to layers of the OSI model; interpret cyberdefense concepts to determine practical implementation methods; formulate and hypothesize how to implement tools and methods in defense of an attack; analyze system compromise activities and mitigations; scrutinize the first principles of network security, including security risk assessment; compare security mechanisms and determine how to implement them in a network; compare and contrast symmetric and asymmetric algorithms used in encryption schemas; analyze technologies and components used to defend networks against security issues to determine priority order in placement; and implement and utilize network monitoring tools.

## 2. BS-2 Defensive Security

### Course Description

The course is designed to prepare students for securing networks from the network administrator's perspective with an emphasis on network security, data and host security, compliance and operation security, access control, identity management, and cryptography. Students will assess cybersecurity risks to networks, evaluate and select appropriate technologies, and apply prevention and detection strategies to defend networks (3 semester hours).

### Course Learning Outcomes (CLO)

Information, cybersecurity, and physical basics; policies and procedures; perimeter defense; network defense; application security; and data defense.

### Student Learning Outcomes (SLO)

Upon completion of the course, students will have acquired the ability to assess basic security measures to the enterprise; explore cybersecurity policies, procedures, and appropriate risk mitigation strategies; apply physical defensive measures for the organization's environment; examine perimeter attacks and appropriate defenses; apply security measures to network hardware; apply various methods to harden hosts and the operating systems; assess networking tools and protocols for access control, authentication, authorization, and other user activities; and evaluate the effectiveness of different encryption methodologies and the best practices of data management.

## 3. BS-3 Firewall and Perimeter Security

### Course Description

The course is designed to enhance the implementation of network perimeter security and will focus on threat vectors and vulnerability assessment, encapsulation at Open Systems Interconnection (OSI), firewall rule bases, Web application and database firewalls, firewall assessment, border routers, intrusion detection and prevention, securing the operating systems and services, baseline audits, forensics, logging, encryption, authentication, wireless network access control, and security tools (3 semester hours).

### Course Learning Outcomes (CLO)

Upon completion of the course, students will have comprehensive knowledge of network security, firewall technology and management, virtual private network (VPN), content filtering, detecting system intrusions, preventing system intrusions, internet security, intranet security, LAN security, wireless security, and RFID security.

### Student Learning Outcomes (SLO)

Upon completion of the course, students will be able to explain how stateful firewalls, proxy firewalls, security policies, and routers are used to implement network security; describe the role of virtual private networks (VPNs); examine how intrusion detection system (IDS) and intrusion prevention systems (IPS) can be used for network defense; appraise host hardening methods and security perimeter designs; utilize subnets and security zones to secure a network; implement wireless network security; analyze network security logs to identify potential threats; interpret postquantum computing cryptographic methods; explain RFID security issues and the relationship of RFID to InfoSec; and examine methods to test a software program's security.

## 4. BS-4 Database Fundamentals

### Course Description

Database Fundamentals examines the fundamental concepts and applications of database systems. Topics include relational database components, database queries, Structured Query Language (SQL), the database life cycle, logical database design using normalization, physical database design, data and process modeling, online transaction processing (OLTP), online analytical processing (OLAP), and extensible markup language (XML). The course explores security concepts and controls to protect databases against cyberattacks (3 semester hours).

### Course Learning Outcomes (CLO)

Core database structures (tables, columns, records); Structured Query Language (SQL); complex queries for data retrieval using joins; database table design and normalization; database access control (users and roles); and database security.

### Student Learning Outcomes (SLO)

Upon completion of the course, students will be able to describe the structure, purpose, and relationships of core database components; compare and contrast current database design models; use relational data modeling tools to design and develop logical database objects; use Structured Query Language (SQL) code to develop and implement database objects and manipulate data; and develop SQL code to implement database security policies.

## 5. BS-5 Principles of Networking Security I

### Course Description

This course provides students with essential knowledge and techniques for securely installing, configuring, maintaining, and troubleshooting a computer network. Students first become familiar with the basics of networking. With the fundamentals in place, the course moves on to cover installing interface cards, managing static and dynamic IP addressing, setting up a wired or wireless network, configuring network security, managing network traffic, and configuring remote access to a network. Students learn how to maintain network security throughout these processes (3 semester hours).

## Course Learning Outcomes (CLO)

Networking basics, cables and connections, networking devices, Ethernet, IP configuration, switch management, routing, firewalls, network customization, wireless networking, wide-area networks (WANs), network policies and procedures, network security, network hardening, network management, and network optimization.

## Student Learning Outcomes (SLO)

Upon completion of the course, students will be able to explain basic networking concepts such as network topologies, the Open Systems Interconnection model (OSI model), network protocols, cables and connectors, network devices, and Ethernet architecture; examine IP addressing and IP services such as Dynamic Host Configuration Protocol (DHCP) and the domain name system (DNS); apply basic management of routing and switching; configure firewalls and customize networks; set up wired and wireless networks; implement elements of network security; apply network management concepts; and implement network optimization concepts.

## 6. BS-6 Principles of Networking Security II

### Course Description

This is a three-credit-hour course in which students are required to submit a well-synthesized ten-page research project with fifteen cited references, due at the end of the semester.

### Course Learning Outcomes (CLO)

Student learning and research guidelines (SLRG); networking basics; cabling, devices, and Ethernet; IP addresses, switch management, and routing; firewalls and customizing networks; wireless networking and wide-area networks; network security and hardening; and network management and optimization.

## Student Learning Outcomes (SLO)

Upon completion of the course, students will be able to take professional certification examinations such as CompTIA A+, Network+, and Security+, among others.

## 7. BS-7 Computer Programming I

### Course Description

The course will focus on learning the fundamentals of computer programming concepts and terminology and on developing simple computer programs. Topics include programming nomenclature, program specification, algorithm development, analysis, problem-solving, and implementation of computer programs. The course also explores application of best practices to develop secure programs. The course will use Python as a base language (3 semester hours).

### Course Learning Outcomes (CLO)

Writing programs in Python; structures that control flow; functions; processing data; exception handling; and object-oriented programming.

### Student Learning Outcomes (SLO)

Upon completion of the course, students will be able to write Python programs and, using variables of data types, use control structures. Using lists, students will be able to write sets, tuples, files, and dictionaries. Students will write modular programs using functions; create programs that process data; implement error and exception handling; and write object-oriented programs.

## 8. BS-8 Fundamentals of Modern Operating Systems

### Course Description

The course will introduce core concepts of modern operating systems. Topics include operating system (OS) nomenclature, OS types, kernels, program execution, memory management, multitasking, device management, virtualization, scheduling, and interaction between computers and the services provided by operating systems hardware. The course also examines key cybersecurity concepts and techniques as applied to modern operating systems (3 semester hours).

### Course Learning Outcomes (CLO)

Implementation of operating systems, operating system structures, processes, threads, process of synchronization, central processing unit (CPU) scheduling, main memory and virtual memory, mass storage structure, file system interface and implementation, input/output (I/O) systems, protection and security, and Linux system.

### Student Learning Outcomes (SLO)

Upon completion of the course, students will be able to classify the various operating system models; analyze the techniques used by operating systems to manage processes; explain how operating systems manage hardware; discuss how network functions are managed within an operating system; discuss how users are managed within an operating system; explain the common techniques used by operating systems for memory management; explain how various mass storage systems work; explain various file management strategies; discuss the role of security and ethics in operating system design and operation; and examine a current operating system implementation.

## 9. BS-9 Routing and Switching Fundamentals

### Course Description

The course will explore basic network operations as they pertain to routing and switching technologies. The course and labs explore the fundamentals of networking, LAN switching technologies, IPv4 and IPv6 routing technologies, WAN technologies, infrastructure services, infrastructure security, and infrastructure management (3 semester hours).

### Course Learning Outcomes (CLO)

Network fundamentals, OSI and TCP/IP models, IPv4 and IPv6 addressing, routing and LAN switching technologies, IP services, device configuration and management, ICND2, advanced switching and routing, wide-area networks, IPv4 and IPv6 routing protocols, infrastructure services, security, and management.

### Student Learning Outcomes (SLO)

Upon completion of the course, students will be able to explain how network traffic operates at various layers of the OSI model; differentiate networking protocols within the TCP/IP protocol suite, including routing and switching protocols; implement network addressing on different devices; use the Cisco IOS to configure, verify, and troubleshoot devices on the network; configure, verify, and troubleshoot VLAN routing; configure, verify, and troubleshoot interswitch connectivity; configure, verify, and troubleshoot WAN interfaces and connectivity; perform network management tasks' and design, implement, and administer networks in a secure system.

## 10. BS-10 Linux Operating System

### Course Description

The course will provide students with a comprehensive overview of the fundamentals of the Linux operating system. Topics covered in the course include system architecture and history, system installation and configuration, the command line interface and shell commands, basic system administration, system updates, file systems, access controls, network services configuration, printer configuration, system services, security models, and scripting (3 semester hours).

## Course Learning Outcomes (CLO)

Linux operating system architecture, use cases, and general background; Linux system installation and configuration; the command line interface and shell commands; basic system administration and system updates; network services and printer configuration; Linux system services and security; editing files and scripting (shell, Bash as an implementation of shell, Perl, Python); and user accounts, user groups, user ownerships, and user permissions access controls (AC).

## Student Learning Outcomes (SLO)

Upon completion of the course, students will be able to describe the Linux community and careers in open sourcing; use simple Linux commands to create directories, to create files, and to get help; execute functions and tasks with commands and scripts; examine the Linux operating system architecture and its differences from other operating systems such as Windows and Unix; establish and maintain security controls for users, tools, applications, and file system permissions on the Linux operating system; and install, configure, and maintain a Linux operating system on a desktop or server.

## 11. BS-11 Defensive and Offensive Ethical Hacking

### Course Description

The course is designed to provide students with an understanding of the approach hackers take in compromising a system. This approach is the same for criminal hackers as it is for ethical hackers, also known as penetration testers. The course examines hacking tools and techniques used by security professionals and ethical hackers to protect an organization's systems and data. It includes topics such as attack vectors, honeypots, penetration testing, and security baseline analyzers.

**Course Learning Outcomes (CLO)**

An introduction to all types of defensive and offensive hackers, ethical hacking concepts, the ordered steps and phases in a hack, specific tools that can be used in each phase of an attack, social engineering, active and passive techniques, sniffing, scanning, gaining access, and hiding evidence.

**Student Learning Outcomes (SLO)**

Upon completion of the course, students will be able to process the activities related to each hacking phase, employ hacking tools to conduct reconnaissance, investigate the security posture of a system using ethical hacking, compare the types of hackers, and determine the appropriate tools to use in the appropriate phases.

## 12. BS-12 Digital Forensics: Techniques and Practices

**Course Description**

The course will explore foundational concepts, tools, and techniques of digital forensics investigations and will investigate violations of company policies, loss of proprietary information, and cybercrimes from a forensics perspective. The goal is to employ appropriate forensic response techniques to support investigations of cyberincidents involving various digital technologies; apply forensic best practices to the collection, handling, and analysis of digital evidence; and report technical and investigative findings in an accurate and ethical manner (3 semester hours).

**Course Learning Outcomes (CLO)**

Forensic data acquisition; crime scene and incident scene processing; current forensic tools; forensics analysis and validation; virtual machine forensics; email, social media, and mobile forensics; cloud forensics; and forensics policies, procedures, and reporting.

## Student Learning Outcomes (SLO)

Upon completion of the course, students will be able to demonstrate the use of various forensic tools; conduct digital investigations from the initial recognition of an incident through the steps of evidence gathering, preservation, and analysis; analyze major components of the NTFS and EX2 file systems and associated forensic artifacts; discover the latest trends in digital forensics including IoT, mobile, cloud, SSD, and virtual machine forensics; explore the rules, laws, policies, and procedures that affect digital forensics; and prepare reports that describe the technical procedures used in forensic investigations.

## 13. BS-13 Wireless and Mobile Networking

### Course Description

The course will provide students with an in-depth study of technologies used to implement wireless and mobile networks in a secure manner. Topics covered include wireless network components; types of wireless networks; network protocols; network performance and management; mobile systems and devices; nomenclature and implementation of mobile computing; mobile operating systems; cellular 3G, 4G, LTE, and 5G networks; and mobile device management. The course also assesses security risks to mobile and wireless technologies and explores the application of appropriate security controls (3 semester hours).

### Course Learning Outcomes (CLO)

Modern wireless and mobile networks; long-term evolution (4G LTE); 5G; small cells, security, and privacy; WPAN, WLAN, and Wi-Fi; WiMAX and WRAN; Internet of Things architecture and security; SS7/C7, signaling, and security; and wireless and mobile security.

**Student Learning Outcomes (SLO)**

Upon completion of the course, students will be able to compare and contrast various mobile networks; examine the use of long-term evolution (LTE) architecture in system evolution, network discovery, and security; analyze advanced mobile architecture such as 5G and small cells; investigate wireless networks from close-distance to wide-area regional networks; analyze Internet of Things (IoT) networks, radio frequency identification (RFID), and near-field communication (NFC); and evaluate cloud, network virtualization, and wireless security.

## 14. BS-14 Critical Infrastructure Security

### Course Description

The course will expand student knowledge of cybersecurity principles and tools related to critical infrastructure. The course investigates and applies digital security frameworks to various types of utility networks and systems such as information technology (IT), industrial control systems (ICSs), supervisory control and data acquisition (SCADA) systems, grids, and distributed networks (3 semester hours).

### Course Learning Outcomes (CLO)

Definition and history of industrial control systems (ICSs), supervisory systems control, and data acquisition (SCADA) systems; practical steps to protect ICSs and SCADA systems; policies, procedures, and frameworks related to ICSs and SCADA systems; threat actors specific to ICSs and SCADA systems; practical application of security to ICS or SCADA; user authentication and authorization; detecting cyberattacks on SCADA systems; and vulnerability assessment.

### Student Learning Outcomes (SLO)

Upon completion of the course, students will be able to use and apply programmable logic controllers in automation; examine the components and applications of industrial control systems; compare various control schemes and their differences; evaluate and implement security functionality across an industrial network; analyze and interpret vulnerabilities associated with industrial control systems; scrutinize, discriminate, and recommend the best practices for different industrial control systems; critique industrial control system policies; and formulate and hypothesize about the most credible threats to industrial control systems.

## 15. BS-15 Cybersecurity Risk Analysis and Management

### Course Description

The course introduces the fundamentals of cybersecurity risk analysis and management, including threat and vulnerability identification/analysis, threat modeling, impact analysis, mitigation planning, and tracking, along with conceptual approaches, guidelines, standards, and security control frameworks. The course includes identification and classification of information assets, formulation of comprehensive risk assessments, and development of threat models and corresponding security plans to serve as frameworks for implementing measures aimed at protecting information assets and reducing security risks (3 semester hours).

### Course Learning Outcomes (CLO)

Evolution of thought regarding cybersecurity risk, cybersecurity risk as a business risk component, risk decisions, leveraging; risk models and life cycles; cybersecurity frameworks, standards, risk assessment, analysis, and evaluation methods and techniques; risk versus compliance; designing and executing mitigation strategies and plans; communicating risk to audiences; and risk management programs.

### Student Learning Outcomes (SLO)

Upon completion of the course, students will be able to articulate the importance of assessing and managing cybersecurity risk within an organization or company; examine key concepts, components, and supporting models and standards of a cybersecurity risk management program; utilize techniques for identifying and analyzing relevant threats, vulnerabilities, and exploits; integrate risk management laws of compliance, standards, best practices, and policies into organizational risk management activities; create and implement a cybersecurity risk mitigation strategy with supporting plans; communicate risk mitigation strategies to senior/executive leadership; and defend an organizational or corporate cybersecurity risk program with supporting plans including business continuity, disaster recovery, and incident response.

## 16. BS-16 Cybersecurity Policies, Programs, and Compliance

### Course Description

The course will examine the application of cybersecurity frameworks, standards, and best practices for enterprise-level policies, plans, and programs. The course also explores formulating security policies and plans, assessing regulatory and ethical aspects of cybersecurity, developing performance metrics for cybersecurity programs, and planning audits of compliance practices and processes (3 semester hours).

### Course Learning Outcomes (CLO)

Information security strategy, information security policies, risk assessment and management, data protection, security audit and compliance (HIPAA, PCI-DSS, FISMA, FERPA, SOX, and GLBA), and information security metrics.

### Student Learning Outcomes (SLO)

Upon completion of the course, students will be able to develop an information security strategy; examine information security policies, policy governance, and ethical aspects; evaluate risk management objectives and response recommendations; analyze data protection requirements and implementation; examine security compliance management and auditing; and prepare information security metrics and key performance indicators.

## 17. BS-17 Cybersecurity Capstone

### Course Description

This is a project-driven study with an emphasis on integration and application of cybersecurity knowledge and skills gained throughout the program. The aim is to examine the architecture of a complex system, identify significant vulnerabilities and threats, and apply appropriate security technologies and methods to ensure the overall security of the system. Advanced cybersecurity principles and best practices are applied to develop a comprehensive cyberdefense program for an enterprise against cyberthreats (3 semester hours).

### Course Learning Outcomes (CLO)

Regulatory concerns, risk management, vulnerability management, access control, physical security, disaster recovery, personnel security, auditing, communication and media protections, configuration management, patch management, incident response, security awareness, security plan contents and requirements, security plan implementation, corporate buy-in management, personnel and corporate culture, and resistance to change.

### Student Learning Outcomes (SLO)

Upon completion of the course, students will be able to analyze the requirements of a comprehensive security plan for an organization; apply cybersecurity principles and methods to defend an information system against cyberthreats; integrate best practices and technologies to develop a security plan for a specific organization; design and customize a comprehensive security plan by integrating network defense tools and measures; examine legal, ethical, and compliance aspects of cybersecurity; evaluate the components of an organization's computing environment; and implement a security plan for an organization.

## 18. BS-18 Network Forensics Investigation and Inquiry

### Course Description

The course will investigate networks from a digital forensics' perspective. It explores application of techniques used in forensic investigations to collect and analyze information from computer networks in response to network intrusions. The course includes analysis of network traffic, identification of threats and vulnerabilities, and evaluation of effects on the system (3 semester hours).

### Course Learning Outcomes (CLO)

Capturing, storing, and analyzing network activity; network forensics as related to incident response and investigation; network forensic capabilities to improve network performance; and network forensic tools and their utility.

### Student Learning Outcomes (SLO)

Upon completion of the course, students will be able to describe potential system attacks and the actors who might perform them; compare and contrast the resources and motivations of bad actors in cyberspace; examine the architecture of a system in order to identify vulnerabilities and risks; determine the appropriate measures to respond to a system compromise; analyze common security failures; track the packets involved in a simple TCP connection or a trace of such a connection; and use a network monitoring tool and network mapping tool to investigate a suspected compromise.

## 19. BS-19 Cloud Computing

### Course Description

The course will examine frameworks and techniques used to design, develop, and implement cloud computing systems. Emphasis is on applied and project-based learning approach to set up Windows-based clouds using client portals, servers, virtual machines, and the accompanying network infrastructure (3 semester hours).

### Course Learning Outcomes (CLO)

History, influences, and challenges of cloud computing; virtualization components and platforms; cloud services (SaaS, PaaS, DaaS, IaaS); service-oriented architectures; deployment models (private, public, community, hybrid); and cybersecurity storage and performance.

### Student Learning Outcomes (SLO)

Upon completion of the course, students will be able to outline the history of the creation and growth of the cloud, including the expansion of cloud service providers; compare the three common cloud service delivery models; identify challenges to cloud computing and recommend mitigation techniques; implement cloud virtualization components (hypervisor, virtual machine [VM], and virtualized infrastructure); manage and improve the performance and storage capability of a cloud network; delineate the components of the cloud's network infrastructure; and use best practices from the cybersecurity industry to provide defense-in-depth to cloud services.

## 20. BS-20 Counterterrorism: Constitutional and Legislative Issues

### Course Description

The course will enhance the student's ability to explore the evolution of homeland security as a concept, a legal framework, and a redirection of national policies and priorities. The political, economic, and practical issues of implementation are examined. The course provides an overview of the history of the terrorist threat and of the United States' responses, and an introduction to fundamental policy legislation and documents, such as national security strategies, US Department of Homeland Security decision directives, the National Response Plan, and the National Incident Management System. The Department of Homeland Security model of planning for, protecting against, responding to, and recovering from a natural disaster and terrorist attacks is also described (3 semester hours).

### Course Learning Outcomes (CLO)

Homeland security: prevention and preparedness, terrorist threats, global terrorism, and balancing security, liberty, and human rights.

### Student Learning Outcomes (SLO)

Upon completion of the course, students will be able to analyze the current terrorist threat to the United States; assess lone wolf attacks and the ability to stop them; differentiate between the investigative tools available to combat terrorism; assess various imminent global terror threats and organizations; differentiate between the types of terrorist groups; evaluate the process of "criminal profiling" terrorists and suspected terrorist groups; examine radical Islam and its various suborganizations; recommend detailed and concrete solutions regarding the war on terrorism; evaluate the legality and effectiveness of FISA courts and FISA warrants; evaluate the making of terrorists, terrorism, and the United States' post-9/11 national security strategy; evaluate the investigative tools used in counterterrorism; and assess Homeland Security concerns such as prevention and preparedness and current trends in terrorism.

## 21. BS-21 Cybersecurity Leadership Overview for Technology and Nontechnology Administrators

### Course Description

Cybersecurity is a source of frustration for public and private organizations and administrators of institutions of higher education who spend an inordinate amount of time and worry trying to protect their data from sophisticated phishing schemes, ransomware, crackers, and hacking. In today's landscape of escalating cybercrime, cybersecurity is not the information technology (IT) team's responsibility but is a universal battle for global citizens. Crackers' and hackers' schemes are the security risks requiring active engagement of technical and nontechnical management officials.

### Course Learning Outcomes (CLO)

The course is designed to provide administrators of public and private organizations and administrators of institutions of higher education with frameworks to battle everyday cybersecurity-related risks. Overall cybersecurity awareness instruction includes the role played by nontechnology employees in matters related to cyberthreats and cyberattacks, systems administration, digital forensics engineering, digital security project management, information assurance, computer programming, cyber-risk, and cyberintelligence.

## 22. BS-22 Introduction to Cybersecurity

### Course Description

Introduction to Cybersecurity provides an introductory study of cybersecurity terminology, principles, and technologies. Fundamental topics covered include cyberthreats and vulnerabilities, information security frameworks, network infrastructure security, wireless network security, cryptography, defense-in-depth security strategy, information security policy, and security management. The goal is to develop a foundation for further study in cybersecurity (3 semester hours).

### Course Learning Outcomes (CLO)

Fundamental concepts of cyberdefense, identification of cyberdefense tools, methodology, security mechanisms, technical and personnel-driven cyberthreats, symmetric and asymmetric algorithms used in encryption schemas, and implementation of secure architecture and infrastructures.

### Student Learning Outcomes (SLO)

Upon completing this course, students will have acquired the expertise to examine and identify threat agents and bad actors to networks, including those involved in cyberterrorism and industrial espionage; analyze defense-in-depth as it relates to layers of the OSI model; interpret cyberdefense concepts to determine practical implementation methods; formulate and hypothesize how to implement tools and methods in defense of an attack; analyze system compromise activities and mitigations; scrutinize the first principles of network security, including security risk assessment; compare security mechanisms and determine how to implement them in a network; compare and contrast symmetric and asymmetric algorithms used in encryption schemas; analyze technologies and components used to defend networks against security issues to determine priority order in placement; and implement and utilize network monitoring tools.

## 23. BS-23 Defensive Security

### Course Description

The course is designed to prepare students for securing networks from the network administrator's perspective with an emphasis on network security, data and host security, compliance and operation security, access control, identity management, and cryptography. Students will assess cybersecurity risks to networks, evaluate and select appropriate technologies, and apply prevention and detection strategies to defend networks (3 semester hours).

### Course Learning Outcomes (CLO)

Information, cybersecurity, and physical basics; policies and procedures; perimeter defense; network defense; application security; and data defense.

### Student Learning Outcomes (SLO)

Upon completion of the course, students will have acquired the ability to assess basic security measures to the enterprise; explore cybersecurity policies, procedures, and appropriate risk mitigation strategies; apply physical defensive measures for the organization's environment; examine perimeter attacks and appropriate defenses; apply security measures to network hardware; apply various methods to harden hosts and the operating systems; assess networking tools and protocols for access control, authentication, authorization, and other user activities; and evaluate the effectiveness of different encryption methodologies and the best practices of data management.

## 24. BS-24 Firewall and Perimeter Security

### Course Description

The course is designed to enhance the implementation of network perimeter security and will focus on threat vectors and vulnerability assessment, encapsulation at Open Systems Interconnection (OSI), firewall rule bases, Web application and database firewalls, firewall assessment, border routers, intrusion detection and prevention, securing the operating systems and services, baseline audits, forensics, logging, encryption, authentication, wireless network access control, and security tools (3 semester hours).

### Course Learning Outcomes (CLO)

Network security, firewall technology and management, virtual private network (VPN), content filtering, detecting system intrusions, preventing system intrusions, internet security, intranet security, LAN security, wireless security, and RFID security.

### Student Learning Outcomes (SLO)

Upon completion of the course, students will be able to explain how stateful firewalls, proxy firewalls, security policies, and routers are used to implement network security; describe the role of virtual private networks (VPNs); examine how an intrusion detection system (IDS) and intrusion prevention system (IPS) can be used for network defense; appraise host hardening methods and security perimeter designs; utilize subnets and security zones to secure a network; implement wireless network security; analyze network security logs to identify potential threats; interpret postquantum computing cryptographic methods; explain RFID security issues and RFID's relationship to InfoSec; and examine methods to test a software program's security.

## 25. BS-25 Database Fundamentals

### Course Description

This course examines the fundamental concepts and applications of database systems. Topics include relational database components, database queries, Structured Query Language (SQL), the database life cycle, logical database design using normalization, physical database design, data and process modeling, online transaction processing (OLTP), online analytical processing (OLAP), and extensible markup language (XML). The course explores security concepts and controls to protect databases against cyberattacks (3 semester hours).

### Course Learning Outcomes (CLO)

Core database structures (tables, columns, records); Structured Query Language (SQL); complex queries for data retrieval using joins; database table design and normalization; database access control (users and roles); and database security.

### Student Learning Outcomes (SLO)

Upon completion of the course, students will be able to describe the structure, purpose, and relationships of core database components; compare and contrast current database design models; use relational data modeling tools to design and develop logical database objects; use Structured Query Language (SQL) code to develop and implement database objects and manipulate data; and develop SQL code to implement database security policies.

## 26. BS-26 Principles of Networking Security I

### Course Description

This course provides students with essential knowledge and techniques for securely installing, configuring, maintaining, and troubleshooting a computer network. Students first become familiar with the basics of networking. With the fundamentals in place, the course moves on to cover installing interface cards, managing static and dynamic IP addressing, setting up a wired or wireless network, configuring network security, managing network traffic, and configuring remote access to a network. Students learn how to maintain network security throughout these processes (3 semester hours).

**Course Learning Outcomes (CLO)**

Networking basics, cables and connections, networking devices, Ethernet, IP configuration, switch management, routing, firewalls, network customization, wireless networking, wide-area networks (WANs), network policies and procedures, network security, network hardening, network management, and network optimization.

**Student Learning Outcomes (SLO)**

Upon completion of the course, students will be able to explain basic networking concepts such as network topologies, the Open Systems Interconnection model (OSI model), network protocols, cables and connectors, network devices, and Ethernet architecture. Students will examine IP addressing and IP services such as Dynamic Host Configuration Protocol (DHCP) and the domain name system (DNS); apply basic management of routing and switching; configure firewalls and customize networks; set up wired and wireless networks; implement elements of network security; apply network management concepts; and implement network optimization concepts.

## 27. BS-27 Principles of Networking Security II

**Course Description**

This is a three-credit-hour course in which students are required to submit a well-synthesized ten-page research project with fifteen cited references, due at the end of the semester.

**Course Learning Outcomes (CLO)**

Student learning and research guidelines (SLRG); networking basics; cabling, devices, and Ethernet; IP addresses, switch management, and routing; firewalls and customizing networks; wireless networking and wide-area networks; network security and hardening; and network management and optimization.

## Student Learning Outcomes (SLO)

Upon completion of the course, students will be able to take professional certification examinations such as CompTIA A+, Network+, and Security+, among others.

## 28. BS-28 Computer Programming I

### Course Description

The course will focus on learning the fundamentals of computer programming concepts and terminology and on developing simple computer programs. Topics include programming nomenclature, program specification, algorithm development, analysis, problem-solving, and implementation of computer programs. The course also explores application of best practices to develop secure programs. The course will use Python as a base language (3 semester hours).

### Course Learning Outcomes (CLO)

Writing programs in Python, structures that control flow, functions, processing data, exception handling, and object-oriented programming.

### Student Learning Outcomes (SLO)

Upon completion of the course, students will be able to write Python programs and, using variables of data types, use control structures. Using lists, sets, tuples, files, and dictionaries, students will write modular programs using functions; create programs that process data; implement error and exception handling; and write object-oriented programs.

## 29. BS-29 Fundamentals of Modern Operating Systems

### Course Description

The course will introduce core concepts of modern operating systems. Topics include operating systems (OS) nomenclature, OS types, kernels, program execution, memory management, multitasking, device management, virtualization, scheduling, and interaction between computers and the services provided by operating systems hardware. The course also examines key cybersecurity concepts and techniques as applied to modern operating systems (3 semester hours).

### Course Learning Outcomes (CLO)

Implementation of operating systems; operating system structures; processes; threads; process of synchronization; central processing unit (CPU) scheduling; main memory and virtual memory; mass storage structure; file system interface and implementation; input/output (I/O) systems; protection and security; and Linux system.

### Student Learning Outcomes (SLO)

Upon completion of the course, students will be able to classify the various operating system models, analyze the techniques used by operating systems to manage processes, explain how operating systems manage hardware, discuss how network functions are managed within an operating system, discuss how users are managed within an operating system, explain the common techniques used by operating systems for memory management, explain how various mass storage systems work, explain various file management strategies, discuss the role of security and ethics in operating system design and operation, and examine a current operating system implementation.

## 30. BS-30 Routing and Switching Fundamentals

### Course Description

The course will explore basic network operations as they pertain to routing and switching technologies. The course and labs explore the fundamentals of networking, LAN switching technologies, IPv4 and IPv6 routing technologies, WAN technologies, infrastructure services, infrastructure security, and infrastructure management (3 semester hours).

### Course Learning Outcomes (CLO)

Network fundamentals, OSI and TCP/IP models, IPv4 and IPv6 addressing, routing and LAN switching technologies, IP services, device configuration and management, ICND2, advanced switching and routing, wide-area networks, IPv4 and IPv6 routing protocols, infrastructure services, security, and management.

### Student Learning Outcomes (SLO)

Upon completion of the course, students will be able to explain how network traffic operates at various layers of the OSI model; differentiate networking protocols within the TCP/IP protocol suite, including routing and switching protocols; implement network addressing on different devices; use the Cisco IOS to configure, verify, and troubleshoot devices on the network; configure, verify, and troubleshoot VLAN routing; configure, verify, and troubleshoot inters witch connectivity; configure, verify, and troubleshoot WAN interfaces and connectivity; perform network management tasks; and design, implement, and administer networks in a secure manner.

## 31. BS-31 Linux Operating System

### Course Description

The course will provide students with comprehensive knowledge to address the fundamentals of the Linux operating system. Topics covered in the course include system architecture and history, system installation and configuration, the command line interface and shell commands, basic system administration, system updates, file systems, access controls, network services configuration, printer configuration, system services, security models, and scripting (3 semester hours).

## Course Learning Outcomes (CLO)

Linux operating system architecture, use cases, and general background; Linux system installation and configuration; the command line interface and shell commands; basic system administration and system updates; network services and printer configuration; Linux system services and security; editing files and scripting (shell, Bash as an implementation of shell, Perl, Python); user accounts; user groups; user ownerships; and user permissions access controls (AC).

## Student Learning Outcomes (SLO)

Upon completion of the course, students will be able to describe the Linux community and careers in open sourcing; use simple Linux commands to create directories, to create files, and to get help; execute functions and tasks with commands and scripts; examine the Linux operating system architecture and its differences from other operating systems such as Windows and Unix; establish and maintain security controls for users, tools, applications, and file system permissions on the Linux operating system; and install, configure, and maintain a Linux operating system on a desktop or server.

## 32. BS-32 Defensive and Offensive Ethical Hacking

## Course Description

The course is designed to provide students with an understanding of the approach hackers take in compromising a system. This approach is the same for criminal hackers as it is for ethical hackers, also known as penetration testers. The course examines hacking tools and techniques used by security professionals and ethical hackers to protect an organization's systems and data. It includes topics such as attack vectors, honeypots, penetration testing, and security baseline analyzers.

## Course Learning Outcomes (CLO)

An introduction to all types of defensive and offensive hackers, ethical hacking concepts, the ordered steps and phases in a hack, specific tools that can be used in each phase of an attack, social engineering, active and passive techniques, sniffing, scanning, gaining access, and hiding evidence.

## Student Learning Outcomes (SLO)

Upon completion of the course, students will be able to process the activities related to each hacking phase, employ hacking tools to conduct reconnaissance, investigate the security posture of a system using ethical hacking, compare the types of hackers, and determine the appropriate tools to use in the appropriate phases.

## 33. BS-33 Digital Forensics: Techniques and Practices

## Course Description

The course explores foundational concepts, tools, and techniques of digital forensics investigations and investigates violations of company policy, loss of proprietary information, and cybercrimes from a forensics perspective. The goal is to employ appropriate forensic response techniques to support investigations of cyberincidents involving various digital technologies; apply forensic best practices to the collection, handling, and analysis of digital evidence; and report technical and investigative findings in an accurate and ethical manner (3 semester hours).

## Course Learning Outcomes (CLO)

Forensic data acquisition; crime scene and incident scene processing; current forensic tools; forensics analysis and validation; virtual machine forensics; email, social media, and mobile forensics; cloud forensics; and forensics policies, procedures, and reporting.

## Student Learning Outcomes (SLO)

Upon completion of the course, students will be able to demonstrate the use of various forensic tools; conduct digital investigations from the initial recognition of an incident through the steps of evidence gathering, preservation, and analysis; analyze major components of the NTFS and EX2 file systems and associated forensic artifacts; discover the latest trends in digital forensics, including IoT, mobile, cloud, SSD, and virtual machine forensics; explore the rules, laws, policies, and procedures that affect digital forensics; and prepare reports that describe the technical procedures used in forensic investigations.

## 34. BS-34 Wireless and Mobile Networking

### Course Description

The course will provide students with an in-depth study of technologies used to implement wireless and mobile networks in a secure manner. Topics covered include wireless network components; types of wireless networks; network protocols; network performance and management; mobile systems and devices; nomenclature and implementation of mobile computing; mobile operating systems; cellular 3G, 4G, LTE, and 5G networks; and mobile device management. The course also assesses security risks to mobile and wireless technologies and explores the application of appropriate security controls (3 semester hours).

### Course Learning Outcomes

Modern wireless and mobile networks; long-term evolution (4G LTE); 5G; small cells, security, and privacy; WPAN, WLAN, and Wi-Fi; WiMAX and WRAN; Internet of Things architecture and security; SS7/C7, signaling, and security; and wireless and mobile security.

### Student Learning Outcomes (SLO)

Upon completion of the course, students will be able to compare and contrast various mobile networks; examine the use of long-term evolution (LTE) architecture in system evolution, network discovery, and security; analyze advanced mobile architecture such as 5G and small cells; investigate wireless networks from close-distance to wide-area regional networks; analyze Internet of Things (IoT) networks, radio frequency identification (RFID), and near-field communication (NFC); and evaluate cloud, network virtualization, and wireless security.

## 35. BS-35 Critical Infrastructure Security

### Course Description

The course will expand student knowledge of cybersecurity principles and tools related to critical infrastructure. The course investigates and applies digital security frameworks to various types of utility networks and systems such as information technology (IT), industrial control systems (ICSs), supervisory control and data acquisition (SCADA) systems, grids, and distributed networks (3 semester hours).

### Course Learning Outcomes (CLO)

Definition and history of industrial control systems (ICSs) and supervisory control and data acquisition (SCADA) systems; practical steps to protect ICSs and SCADA systems; policy, procedures, and frameworks related to ICSs and SCADA systems; threat actors specific to ICSs and SCADA systems; practical application of security to ICS and SCADA; user authentication and authorization; detecting cyberattacks on SCADA systems; and vulnerability assessment.

### Student Learning Outcomes (SLO)

Upon completion of the course, students will be competent in the use and application of programmable logic controllers in automation. Students will examine the components and applications of industrial control systems; compare various control schemes and their differences; evaluate and implement security functionality across an industrial network; analyze and interpret vulnerabilities associated with industrial control systems; scrutinize, discriminate, and recommend the best practices for different industrial control systems; critique industrial control system policies; and formulate and hypothesize about the most credible threats to industrial control systems.

## 36. BS-36 Cybersecurity Risk Analysis and Management

### Course Description

The course introduces the fundamentals of cybersecurity risk analysis and management, including threat and vulnerability identification/analysis, threat modeling, impact analysis, and mitigation planning and tracking. The course also discusses conceptual approaches, guidelines, standards, and security control frameworks. The course includes identification and classification of information assets, formulation of comprehensive risk assessments, development of threat models, and development of corresponding security plans to serve as frameworks for implementing measures aimed at protecting information assets and reducing security risks (3 semester hours).

## Course Learning Outcomes (CLO)

Evolution of thought regarding cybersecurity risk, cybersecurity risk as a business risk component, risk decisions, and leveraging; risk models and life cycles; cybersecurity frameworks, standards, risk assessment, analysis, and evaluation methods and techniques; risk versus compliance; designing and executing mitigation strategies and plans; and communicating risk to audiences and risk management programs.

## Student Learning Outcomes (SLO)

Upon completion of the course, students will be able to articulate the importance of assessing and managing cybersecurity risk within an organization or company; examine key concepts, components, supporting models, and standards of a cybersecurity risk management program; utilize techniques for identifying and analyzing relevant threats, vulnerabilities, and exploits; integrate risk management laws of compliance, standards, best practices, and policies into organizational risk management activities; create and implement a cybersecurity risk mitigation strategy with supporting plans; communicate risk mitigation strategies to senior/executive leadership; and defend an organizational or corporate cybersecurity risk program with supporting plans, including business continuity, disaster recovery, and incident response.

## 37. BS-37 Cybersecurity Policies, Programs, and Compliance

## Course Description

The course will examine the application of cybersecurity frameworks, standards, and best practices to enterprise-level policies, plans, and programs.

The course also explores formulating security policies and plans, assessing regulatory and ethical aspects of cybersecurity, developing performance metrics for cybersecurity programs, and planning audits of compliance practices and processes.

**Course Learning Outcomes (CLO)**

Information security strategy, information security policies, risk assessment and management, data protection, security audit and compliance (HIPAA, PCI-DSS, FISMA, FERPA, SOX, and GLBA), and information security metrics.

**Student Learning Outcomes (SLO)**

Upon completion of the course, students will be able to develop an information security strategy; examine information security policies, policy governance, and ethical aspects; evaluate risk management objectives and response recommendations; analyze data protection requirements and implementation; examine security compliance management and auditing; and prepare information security metrics and key performance indicators.

## 38. BS-38 Cybersecurity Capstone

**Course Description**

This is a project-driven study with an emphasis on integration and application of cybersecurity knowledge and skills gained throughout the program. The aim is to examine the architecture of a complex system, identify significant vulnerabilities and threats, and apply appropriate security technologies and methods to ensure the overall security of the system. Advanced cybersecurity principles and best practices are applied to develop a comprehensive cyberdefense program for an enterprise against cyberthreats (3 semester hours).

**Course Learning Outcomes (CLO)**

Regulatory concerns, risk management, vulnerability management, access control, physical security, disaster recovery, personnel security, auditing, communication and media protections, configuration management, patch management, incident response, security awareness, security plan contents and requirements, security plan implementation, corporate buy-in management, personnel and corporate culture, and resistance to change.

**Student Learning Outcomes (SLO)**

Upon completion of the course, students will be able to analyze the requirements of a comprehensive security plan for an organization; apply cybersecurity principles and methods to defend an information system against cyberthreats; integrate best practices and technologies to develop a security plan for a specific organization; design and customize a comprehensive security plan by integrating network defense tools and measures; examine legal, ethical, and compliance aspects of cybersecurity; evaluate the components of an organization's computing environment; and implement a security plan for an organization.

### 39. BS-39 Network Forensics Investigation and Inquiry

**Course Description**

The course will investigate networks from a digital forensics' perspective. It explores application of techniques used in forensic investigations to collect and analyze information from computer networks in response to network intrusions. The course includes analysis of network traffic, identification of threats and vulnerabilities, and evaluation of effects on the system (3 semester hours).

**Course Learning Outcomes (CLO)**

Capturing, storing, and analyzing network activity; network forensics as related to incident response and investigation; network forensic capabilities to improve network performance; and network forensic tools and their utility.

**Student Learning Outcomes (SLO)**

Upon completion of the course, students will be able to describe potential system attacks and the actors who might perform them; compare and contrast the resources and motivations of bad actors in cyberspace; examine the architecture of a system in order to identify vulnerabilities and risks; determine the appropriate measures to respond to a system compromise; analyze common security failures; track the packets involved in a simple TCP connection or a trace of such a connection; and use a network monitoring tool and network mapping tool to investigate a suspected compromise.

## 40. BS-40 Cloud Computing

### Course Description

The course will examine frameworks and techniques used to design, develop, and implement cloud computing systems. Emphasis is on applied and project-based learning approach to set up Windows-based clouds using client portals, servers, virtual machines, and the accompanying network infrastructure (3 semester hours).

### Course Learning Outcomes (CLO)

History, influences, and challenges of cloud computing; virtualization components and platforms; cloud services (SaaS, PaaS, DaaS, IaaS); service-oriented architectures; deployment models (private, public, community, hybrid); and cybersecurity storage and performance.

### Student Learning Outcomes (SLO)

Upon completion of the course, students will be able to outline the history of the creation and growth of the cloud, including the expansion of cloud service providers; compare and contrast the three common cloud service delivery models; identify challenges to cloud computing and recommend mitigation techniques; implement cloud virtualization components (hypervisor, virtual machine [VM], and virtualized infrastructure); manage and improve the performance and storage capability of a cloud network; delineate the components of the cloud's network infrastructure; and use best practices from the cybersecurity industry to provide defense-in-depth to cloud services.

## 41. BS-41 Counterterrorism: Constitutional and Legislative Issues

### Course Description

The course will enhance the student's ability to explore the evolution of homeland security as a concept, a legal framework, and a redirection of national policies and priorities. The political, economic, and practical issues of implementation are examined. The course provides an overview of the history of the terrorist threat and of the United States' responses, and an introduction to fundamental policy legislation and documents, such as national security strategies, US Department of Homeland Security decision directives, the National Response Plan, and the National Incident Management System. The Department of Homeland Security model of planning for, protecting against, responding to, and recovering from a natural disaster and terrorist attacks is also described (3 semester hours).

## Course Learning Outcomes (CLO)

Homeland security: prevention and preparedness; terrorist threats; global terrorism; and balancing security, liberty, and human rights.

## Student Learning Outcomes (SLO)

Upon completion of the course, students will be able to analyze the current terrorist threat to the United States, assess lone wolf attacks and the ability to stop them, differentiate between the investigative tools available to combat terrorism, assess various imminent global terror threats and organizations, differentiate between the types of terrorist groups, evaluate the process of "criminal profiling" terrorists and suspected terrorist groups, examine radical Islam and its various suborganizations, recommend detailed and concrete solutions regarding the war on terrorism, evaluate the legality and effectiveness of FISA courts and FISA warrants, evaluate the making of terrorists, terrorism, and the United States' post-9/11 national security strategy; assess the investigative tools used in counterterrorism; and become familiar with areas of homeland security such as prevention and preparedness, and current trends in terrorism.

# Graduate (MSc) and Postgraduate (PhD) Studies in Cybersecurity

◇◇◇◇◇◇◇◇◇◇◇◇◇◇◇◇◇◇◇◇◇◇◇◇◇◇◇◇◇◇◇◇◇◇◇◇◇◇◇◇◇◇◇◇◇◇◇◇◇◇◇◇◇◇◇◇◇◇◇

## Formation of Graduate and Postgraduate Studies

The Master of Science in Cybersecurity degree consists of thirty credit hours of graduate-level courses. The first half of this program provides students with a strong foundation in network security, operating systems security, cryptography, and secure software development to prepare them for more advanced courses in the program. The second half of the program focuses on emerging trends and more advanced themes in cybersecurity, including digital forensics, cyber-risk management, cyberincidents response, and cybersecurity strategy, governance, and ethics.

Cybersecurity education is a much-needed natural resource with the competitive advantage to transform public and private organizations, institutions of higher education, and health-care operations across the globe. Equity of cybersecurity in graduate and postgraduate studies is worth practicing; this growing professional field is designed to combat threats to global security. Most course offerings are geared toward the career advancement of security software developers, who often work multiple security features, allowing them to advance as programmers with expertise in the field of cybersecurity, cloud technology, and mobile telecommunications; security architects, who have the ability to oversee the design and implementation of security systems and to analyze security threats; digital forensic investigators, who are empowered with the expertise to track down information related to cybercrime, cyberthreats, and cyberattacks, track the evidence leading to perpetrators of cybercrimes, do a security analysis to find weaknesses and data breaches, and perform digital forensics; information security analysts, with expertise in computer network security, locating vulnerable parts of a computer system, installing protective software, and staying abreast of advancements in computer security; and security engineers, who have expertise in monitoring the security of data and information security and in forensic analysis. Graduate studies in cybersecurity is rigorous, is challenging, and is often fueled by public and private organizations that require candidates with an undergraduate degree in cybersecurity and professional certifications or candidates with an advanced degree in cybersecurity. The continued advancements in technology and the increasing sophistication of perpetrators of cybercrimes, cyberthreats, cyberattacks, and digital data breaches are both steadily advancing to the forefront of private and public organizations, institutions of higher education, the health-care industry, government agencies, and airport authorities, forcing them to step up the aggressive measures to protect their data, information, resources, and assets. The global community must not condone the current apparent massive deficit in cybersecurity; graduate studies in cybersecurity continue to remain the paramount objective. It is true that one seeming shortfall of the cybersecurity profession is the high level of education and in-depth skills required to defend against, protect against, and respond to cyberattacks. The paramount purpose for demanding an advanced education, far-reaching knowledge, and skills in the cybersecurity domain is to equip first responders with the expertise needed to battle all aspects of any Machiavellian cybercriminal strategies.

## Importance of Graduate and Postgraduate Studies

Cybersecurity is an innovative and rapidly growing discipline concerned with offensive, defensive, and protective measures against culprits and with street committees' access to public and private organizations, institutions of higher education, and the health-care system. The internet, our current global network communications, and today's data transmission systems were created predominantly by the military to reinforce around-the-clock security systems. These days, the internet is accessible by everyone, including vulnerable innocent citizens as well as aggressive sophisticated criminals who are forever busy creating active plans of action, willing and ready to launch them. It is worth noting that cybersecurity professionals and law enforcement officers are in competition with cybercriminals who have even a partial education. Without regard for anything but their own gain, these cybercriminals are armed with operationally offensive digital weapons while vulnerable innocent global citizens and law enforcement officers who absolutely do not want to lose the battle are operating with similar digital armaments to defend against, protect against, and withstand these perpetrators.

Citizens and law enforcement officers are strongly encouraged to complete graduate studies in cybersecurity, which will cause them to become well-versed with regard to professional expertise and will give them a strong knowledge base to create, maintain, and protect their organization's digital security databases or, in the case of law enforcement, their numerical and informational databanks. Most cyberthreats and cyberattacks, including denial-of-service attacks (DoSA) and telephony denial-of-service attack (TDoSA), often render nonfunctional an organization's network system and thereby cause the internet connection to become permanently inoperable and unable to respond to legitimate requests from authorized users. This place law enforcement officers in a state of deferment; they are unable to function effectively. Telephony denial-of-service attacks often render an organization's otherwise functional voice system inoperable. Graduate studies in cybersecurity helps a person bridge this gap, going deeper into the subject matter than undergraduate studies and offering unmatched in-depth expertise and skills in different subject areas such as cyberterrorism, spyware, and cybercrime, along with the online forensics' skills required to perform offensive and defensive actions and identify intruders so as to stop them prior to their launching of cyberattacks. Cybersecurity professional with advanced knowledge and skills are greatly in demand today because of the magnitude of the problem of cybercrime and the alarmingly high number of sophisticated and equipped cyberterrorists, hackers, and criminals with an entirely new arsenal of cyberweapons across the globe.

The 2020 COVID-19 pandemic has forced world citizens, many organizations, institutions of higher education, and health-care facilities to adapt a format to minimize health risks, thereby depriving employees, faculty, other educators, students, and clients of the chance to be in close physical contact with one another. This reworked approach has pushed millions of global communities into ensuring limited contact with other people, the wearing of face masks, the implementation of remote working structures, including online interactions between faculty, educators, students, customers, and organizations. At present, these changes in behavior and the reworked methodology must be mitigated, defended, and protected by cybersecurity professionals with the advanced degrees, expertise, credentials, and comprehensive knowledge required to face the challenge of an increased number of requests from individuals and organizational personnel to sidestep and circumvent authorized security best practices and approved telework solutions. This gives bad actors the opening they need to create and delete vital security settings information, engage in phishing, engage in data theft for extortion purposes, create disruptive and destructive ransomware attacks, engage in professional cybercriminal activities, become part of one of a number of cultured cybercriminal gangs, engage in continued espionage, and increase breaches caused by carelessness.

The purpose of equitably integrating an education in cybersecurity into graduate study programs is to ensure that cybersecurity professionals have the intellectual capability and broad-range knowledge needed to battle the increasing number of cybercriminals across the globe.

# Course Offerings:
# Graduate and Postgraduate Studies

◇◇◇◇◇◇◇◇◇◇◇◇◇◇◇◇◇◇◇◇◇◇◇◇◇◇◇◇◇◇◇◇◇◇◇◇◇◇◇◇◇◇◇◇◇◇◇◇◇◇◇◇◇◇◇◇◇◇

### MPH-1 Cybersecurity Foundations

Cybersecurity Foundations covers fundamental concepts of the interdisciplinary field of cybersecurity by taking into consideration both technical and management aspects. Students analyze cyberthreats and vulnerabilities and examine common cyberdefense technologies, processes, and procedures. Students are exposed to how cybersecurity can be enforced in networks, operating systems, software development, and the system development life cycle (SDLC). The course also introduces students to the human, legal, privacy, and ethical aspects of cybersecurity. The goal is to prepare students for advanced study in cybersecurity (3 credits).

### MPH-2 Operating Systems Security

Operating Systems Security covers the fundamentals of the modern operating system (OS), including basic operating system structure, file systems and storage servers, memory management techniques, process scheduling and resource management, threads, and distributed and peer-to-peer systems. OS-level mechanisms and policies to investigate and defend against cyberattacks are evaluated. Applications of OS security techniques, such as authentication, system call monitoring, and memory protection, are explored (3 credits).

### MPH-3 Cryptography and Data Security

Cryptography and Data Security focuses on how cryptographic protocols, tools, and techniques work and how to appropriately apply them to protect data. Topics covered include symmetric cryptography, public key cryptography, hash functions, digital signatures, key management, cryptographic modes, and cryptographic protocols. Different attacks on cryptographic systems are analyzed, and the role of cryptography in data protection, data integrity, privacy, and authentication is thoroughly investigated. Students learn to protect data at rest, in process, and in transition (3 credits).

## MPH-4 Software and Applications Security

Software and Applications Security covers the foundations of software and applications security. Students are exposed to basic programming and software development processes to enable them to understand the risks associated with insecure software. Fundamental secure coding concepts, principles, and techniques to make software more secure and resilient are explored. Software vulnerabilities and attacks such as buffer overflows, SQL injection, and session hijacking are analyzed, and appropriate prevention and mitigation methods such as advanced testing and program analysis techniques are applied (3 credits).

## MPH-5 Cyberforensics and Investigation

Cyberforensics and Investigation covers the fundamental concepts, tools, and techniques of digital forensics and cyberinvestigation. Topics include the identification, preservation, collection, examination, analysis, and presentation of digital evidence for administrative, civil, and criminal investigations. Applications of appropriate tools and technologies used for securing, handling, and preserving digital evidence are explored. The legal and ethical aspects associated with digital forensics and cyberinvestigation are examined in depth (3 credits).

## MPH-6 Principles of Cryptography

The course explores the foundation and techniques of contemporary cryptography to enable cybersecurity professionals to retain the privacy and security of digital data and information. Subject areas involve digital signature, public key infrastructure, symmetric block ciphers, authentication protocols, classical cryptographic techniques, cryptographic protocols, and complex and computational number theories (3 credits).

## MPH-7 Foundation of Digital Forensics

The emphasis of this course is on the identification, extraction, analysis, and preservation of digital evidence stored on computers, network system file servers, and most devices often in connection with criminal investigations, court cases, forensic reporting, data recovery, pattern detection, and file system analysis (3 credits).

## MPH-8 Biometric Algorithm

The course focuses on the use of unique physical characteristic to identify individuals; maintaining data security and privacy; recognition rate; alternatives to passwords; security strength; modern digital biometric techniques; and application to computer and data security (3 credits).

## MPH-9 Cyberintelligence Operations

This course prepares students to learn how to assess security risks on computer hardware, software, and other data; how to identify impending cybercrime, cyberthreats, or cyberattacks; how to gather information on potential perpetrators; and how to mitigate risks and protect computer systems, sensitive data, and other information (3 credits).

## MPH-10 Cyber Risk Management and Incident Response

Cyber Risk Management and Incident Response delves into practical methods and techniques used for assessing and managing cybersecurity risks to an organization. Both quantitative and qualitative risk assessment methodologies are covered. Common cybersecurity risk assessment/management models and frameworks are evaluated and applied. Another major area of focus is cyberincident response and contingency planning, consisting of incident response planning, disaster recovery planning, and business continuity planning (3 credits).

## MPH-11 Cybersecurity Strategy, Governance, and Ethics

Cybersecurity Strategy, Governance, and Ethics is designed to provide the knowledge and skills necessary to design cybersecurity strategy, including people, process, and technology, in a modern enterprise. Students are exposed to cybersecurity policy formulation, governance structures for policy creation, selection and implementation of policy, and audit and control functions to ensure compliance and efficacy. Students also learn to navigate the human, legal, privacy, and ethical aspects of cybersecurity (3 credits).

## MPH-12 Special Topics in Cybersecurity

Special Topics in Cybersecurity explores emerging trends and latest technological advances related to cybersecurity and cyberspace. Special topics related to state-of-the-art cybersecurity, such as cloud computing security, security of the Internet of Things (IoT), security of industrial systems and cyberphysical systems (CPS), prevention and detection of insider threats, supply chain security, and blockchain technology for IT security, are explored. Topics are changed from time to time to reflect the rapidly evolving changes in the field of cybersecurity (3 credits).

## MPH-13 Capstone in Cybersecurity

Capstone in Cybersecurity is an integrative multidisciplinary course that applies the knowledge, skills, and postures gained throughout the program to real-world cybersecurity contexts. Students analyze current cybersecurity problems and develop recommendations to solve the problem(s) and/or mitigate the impact. Students apply best practices and appropriate technologies to design, implement, manage, assess, and further enhance information security in a modern enterprise (3 credits).

## MPH-14 Information Security Policy Governance

The course explores the full spectrum of information security: threats, software vulnerabilities, programming for malice, basic cryptography, operating system protections, network security, privacy, data mining, computer crime, governance, cyberthreats, cybersecurity management, state and national organization public policy, and the digital biometric and internet ecosystem (3 credits).

## MPH-15 Cybersecurity Management Information Security

This course introduces students to the policy and management of cybersecurity, including system concepts, cyberthreats, cybersecurity conflict, and advanced information security studies (3 credits).

# References

Anderson, D., and S. Burns. "One-Minute Paper: Student Perception of Learning Gains." *College Student Journal* 47 (2013): 219–27.

Aquilina, James M., Eoghan Casey, and Cameron Malin. *Malware Forensics: Investigation and Analyzing Malicious Code.* Burlington, MA: Syngress, 2008.

Assenter, M., and D. Tobey. "Enhancing the Cybersecurity Workforce." *IT Professional* 13, no. 1 (2011): 12–15. http://ieeexplore.ieee.org/xpl/freeabs_all.jsp?arnumber=5708280.

Benvenuto, E. *An Introduction to the History of Structural Mechanics.* New York: Springer-Verlag, 1991.

Benton, L. S., D. Duchon, and W. H. Pallett. "Validity of Student Self-Reported Ratings of Learning." *Assessment & Evaluation in Higher Education* 38 (2013): 377–88.

Brown, Cameron S. D. "Investigating and Prosecuting Cyber Crime." *Forensic Dependencies and Barriers to Justice* 9, no. 1 (2015): 55–119.

Chapple, Mike, and David Seidl. *Certified Information Systems Security Professional (CISSP).* Indianapolis: John Wiley & Sons, 2016.

Easton, Chuck, and Jeff Det Taylor. *Computer Crime, Investigation, and the Law.* Boston: Cengage Learning Course Technology, 2011.

Esin, Joseph O. *Landscape of Cybersecurity Threats and Forensic Inquiry.* Bloomington, IN: AuthorHouse, 2017.

———. *System Overview of Cyber-Technology in a Digitally Connected Society.* Bloomington, IN: AuthorHouse, 2017.

Fitzgerald, Alvita, and Jessica Schneider. "Keep It Secret, Keep It Safe: Nine Steps to Maintaining Data Security." *United States Cyber Security Magazine* 3, no. 7 (2015): 74–75.

Ginsberg, M., and R. Wolkowski. *Diversity and Motivation.* San Francisco: Jossey-Bass, 2009.

Givens, Austen D. "Strengthening Cyber Incident Response Capabilities through Education and Training in the Incident Command System." *Journal of the National Cybersecurity Institute* 2, no. 3 (2015): 65–75.

Heckman, Mark R. "Cybersecurity Education's Cargo Cult." *United States Cybersecurity Magazine* 4, no. 10 (2016).

Hammer, D., P. Piascik, M. Medina, A. Pettinger, R. Rose, F. Creekmore, R. Soltis, A. Bouldin, L. Schwarz, and S. Steven. "Recognition of Teaching Excellence." *American Journal of Pharmaceutical Education* 74 (2010): 1–11.

Humphrey, N., P. Bartolo, P. Ale, C. Calleja, T. Hofsaess, V. Janikova, and G. M. Wetso. "Understanding and Responding to Diversity in the Primary Classroom: An International Study." *European Journal of Teacher Education* 29, no. 3 (2006): 305–18.

Komarraju, M., S. Musulkin, and G. Bhattacharya. "Role of Student-Faculty Interactions in Developing College Students' Academic Self-Concept, Motivation, and Achievement." *Journal of College Student Development* 51 (2010): 333–42.

LeClair, Jane, and Sherri W. Ramsay. *Protecting Our Future: Educating a Cybersecurity Workforce.* Albany, NY: Hudson Whitman Excelsior College Press, 2015.

Ngwang, E. N. "Individual Freedom, Cyber Security, and Nuclear Proliferation in a Borderless Land: Innovations and the Trade-Offs in Scientific Progress." *Journal of Educational Research and Technology (JERT)* 5, no. 5 (2016): 33–72.

Paolini, Allison. "Enhancing Teaching Effectiveness and Student Learning Outcomes." *Journal of Effective Teaching* 15, no. 1 (2015): 20–33.

Parker, Charles. "In Support of Cyber/InfoSec Unification." Washington Center for Cybersecurity Center and Development. Washington, DC, 2017.

Shinder, Debra L., and E. Tittel. *Cybercrime: Scene of the Cybercrime Computer Forensics Handbook.* Rockland, MA: Syngress, 2002.

Smith, Christen Marie. "Building the Cyber Force of the Future." *United States Cybersecurity Magazine* 3, no. 9 (2015): 43–55.

# Examinations Bank

Per Esin (2017, 2019), Chapple and Seidi (2016), Harris and Ham (2016), McMillan and Abernathy (2014), and Harris (2008), strengthening of instruction, learning endeavors, and professional certification examinations must be supported.

**Areas of Discipline**

- Access control security
- Cryptography
- Assets security
- Physical security
- Telecommunications and network security
- Legal regulations, investigation, and compliance
- Software development security
- Security architecture and design
- Operations security
- Disaster recovery
- Secure network protocols

## Access Control

1. A network device designed for managing the optional distribution of workloads across multiple computing resources is known as:
    a. layer 3 switch
    b. access point
    c. load balancer
    d. domain controller

2. Which of the terms listed below refers to a method that ignores the load-balancing algorithm by consistently passing a request from a given client to the same server?
   a. round-robin method
   b. active-active configuration
   c. session affinity
   d. least connection method

3. In a round-robin method, each consecutive request is handled by: (Select best answer)
   a. the first server in a cluster
   b. the next server in a cluster
   c. the least-utilized server in a cluster
   d. the last server in a cluster

4. In a weighted round-robin method, each consecutive request is handled in a rotation fashion, but servers with higher specs are designed to process more workload.
   a. True
   b. False

5. In active-passive mode, load balancers distribute network traffic across:
   a. all servers
   b. servers marked as active.
   c. least-utilized servers
   d. servers marked as passive.

6. In active-active mood, load balancers distribute network traffic across:
   a. least-utilized servers
   b. none of the servers
   c. all servers
   d. most-utilized servers

7. An IP address that does not correspond to any actual physical network interface is called a virtual IP address (VIP/VIPA).
   a. True
   b. False

8. What type of IP address would be assigned to a software-based load balancer to handle an internet hosted on several Web servers, each with its own private IP address?
   a. IPv4 address
   b. virtual IP address
   c. non routable IP address
   d. IPv6 address

9. An infrastructure device designed for connecting wireless and/or wired client devices to a network is commonly referred to as:
   a. captive portal
   b. access point
   c. intermediate distribution frame (IDF)
   d. active hub

10. Which of the following initialisms is used as a unique identifier for a WLAN (a wireless network name)?
    a. BSS
    b. SSID
    c. ESS
    d. IBSS

11. Disabling SSD broadcast:
    a. is one of the measures used in securing wireless networks.
    b. makes a WLAN harder to discover.
    c. blocks access to a WAP.
    d. prevents wireless clients from accessing the network.

12. A network security access control method whereby the forty-eight-bit physical address assigned to each network card is used to determine access to the network is known as:
    a. MAC filtering
    b. network address translation
    c. static IP addressing
    d. network access control (NAC)

13. Which of the tools listed below would be of help in troubleshooting signal loss and low wireless network signal coverage?
    a. logical network diagram
    b. protocol analyzer
    c. WAP power-level controls
    d. physical network diagram

14. Frequency bands for IEEE 802.11 networks include: (Select 2 answers.)
    a. 5.0 GHz
    b. 2.4 GHz
    c. 5.4 GHz
    d. 2.0 GHz

15. A common example of channel overlapping in wireless networking could be the 2.4 GHz band used in 802.11 networks, where the 2.401–2.473 GHz frequency range is used for allocating 11 channels, each taking up a 22-MHz portion of the available spectrum. Setting up a wireless network to operate on a nonoverlapping channel (1, 6, and 11 in this case) allows multiple networks to coexist in the same area without causing interference.
    a. True
    b. False

16. Which of the following answers refers to a common antenna type used as a standard equipment on most access points (APs) for indoor wireless local area network (WLAN) deployments?
    a. dipole antenna
    b. dish antenna
    c. unidirectional antenna
    d. Yagi antenna

17. Which of the antenna types listed below provide 360-degree horizontal signal coverage? (Select 2 answers.)
    a. unidirectional antenna
    b. dipole antenna
    c. dish antenna
    d. omnidirectional antenna
    e. Yagi antenna

18. Which of the following answers refers to highly directional antenna types used for long-range point-to-point links? (Select 2 answers.)
    a. dipole antenna
    b. omnidirectional antenna
    c. dish antenna
    d. nondirectional antenna
    e. unidirectional antenna

19. An optimal wireless access point (WAP) antenna placement provides a countermeasure against:
    a. war chalking
    b. tailgating
    c. war driving
    d. shoulder surfing

20. A type of architecture in which most of the network configuration settings of an access point (AP) are set and managed with the use of a central switch or controller is called:
    a. thin AP
    b. infrastructure mode
    c. fat AP
    d. ad hoc mode

21. The term *fat AP* refers to a stand-alone access point (AP) device type offering extended network configuration options that can be set and managed after logging in to the device.
    a. True
    b. False

22. A technology that allows for real-time analysis of security alerts generated by network hardware and applications is known as:
    a. LACP
    b. DSCP
    c. SIEM
    d. LWAPP

23. Which of the following statements describing the functionality of SIEM is not true?
    a. Data can be collected from many different sources.
    b. Collected data can be processed into actionable information.
    c. Automated alerting and triggers are active.
    d. Time synchronization is available.
    e. Event deduplication occurs.
    f. Use of rewritable storage media is recommended.

24. Which of the terms listed below refers to computer data storage systems, data storage devices, and data storage media that can be written to once but read from multiple times?
    a. DVD-RW
    b. tape library
    c. floppy disk
    d. WORM

25. Which of the following initialisms refers to software-or hardware-based security solutions designed to detect and prevent unauthorized use and transmission of confidential information outside the corporate network?
    a. DRP
    b. DHE
    c. DLP
    d. DEP

26. What is the best countermeasure against social engineering?
    a. AAA protocols
    b. user authentication
    c. strong passwords
    d. user education

27. Which of the following violates the principle of least privilege?
    a. onboarding process
    b. improperly configured accounts
    c. shared accounts for privileged users
    d. time-of-day restrictions

28. An e-commerce store app running on an unpatched Web server is an example of:
    a. architecture/design weakness
    b. risk acceptance
    c. vulnerable business process
    d. security through obscurity

29. The purpose of a downgrade attack is to make a computer system fall back to a weaker security mode, which makes the system more vulnerable to attacks.
    a. True
    b. False

30. A situation in which an application fails to properly release memory allocated to it or continually requests more memory than it needs is called:
    a. memory leak
    b. buffer overflow
    c. DLL injection
    d. integer overflow

31. Which of the terms listed below describes a programing error where an application tries to store a numeric value in a variable that is too small to hold it?
    a. buffer overflow
    b. pointer dereferences.
    c. memory leak
    d. integer overflow

32. A situation in which an application writes to an area of memory that it is not supposed to access is referred to as:
    a. DLL injection
    b. buffer overflow
    c. memory leak
    d. integer overflow

33. Which of the following terms describes an attempt to read a variable that stores a null value?
    a. integer overflow
    b. pointer dereferences.
    c. butter overflow
    d. memory leak

34. A collection of precompiled functions designed to be used by more than one Microsoft Windows application simultaneously to save system resources is known as:
    a. DLL
    b. ISO
    c. EXE
    d. INI

35. Which of the terms listed below describes a type of attack that relies on executing a library of code?
    a. memory leak
    b. DLL injection
    c. pointer deference
    d. butter overflow

36. In the IT industry, the term *systems sprawl* is used to describe one of the aspects of a poor asset management process.
    a. True
    b. False

37. An effective asset management process provides countermeasures against: (Select all that apply)
    a. system sprawl
    b. race conditions
    c. undocumented assets
    d. architecture and design weaknesses
    e. user errors

38. Which of the following best describes what a zero-day attack exploits:
    a. new accounts
    b. patched software
    c. a vulnerability that is present in already released software but is unknown to the software developer
    d. a well-known vulnerability

39. A type of software or hardware that checks information coming from the internet and, depending on the applied configuration settings, either blocks it or allows it to pass through is called:
    a. antivirus
    b. firewall
    c. antispyware
    d. malware

40. Which of the following applies to a request that doesn't match the criteria defined in an ACL?
    a. group policy
    b. implicit deny rule
    c. transitive trust
    d. context-aware authentication

41. Stateless inspection is a firewall technology that keeps track of network connections and, based on the collected data, determines which network packets should be allowed through the firewall.
    a. True
    b. False

42. Which of the answers listed below refers to a dedicated device for managing encrypted connections established over an untrusted network, such as the internet?
    a. VNP concentrator
    b. load balancer
    c. managed switch
    d. multilayer switch

43. VPNs can be either remote access (used for connecting networks) or site-to-site (used for connecting a computer to a network).
    a. True
    b. False

44. Which of the IPsec modes provides entire packet encryption?
    a. tunnel
    b. payload
    c. transport
    d. default

45. An IPsec mode providing encryption only for the payload (the data part of the packet) is known as:
    a. protected mode
    b. tunnel mode
    c. transport mode
    d. safe mode

46. Which part of the IPsec protocol provides authentication and integrity?
    a. CRC
    b. AH
    c. SIEM
    d. AES

47. Which of the IPsec protocols provides authentication, integrity, and confidentiality?
    a. AES
    b. SHA
    c. AH
    d. ESP

48. Which of the terms listed below describes a type of VPN that alleviates bottlenecks and conserves bandwidth by allowing users simultaneously to make use of both the VPN and public network links?
    a. tethering
    b. split tunnel
    c. load balancing
    d. full tunnel

49. Examples of secure VPN tunneling protocols include: (Select 2 answers.)
    a. crypts
    b. SCP
    c. IPsec
    d. WEP
    e. TLS

50. The term *always-on VPN* refers to a type of persistent VPN connection the starts automatically as soon as the computer detects a network link.
    a. True
    b. False

51. Which security principle is the opposite of disclosure?
    a. integrity
    b. availability
    c. confidentiality
    d. authorization

52. Which of the following is *not* an example of a knowledge authentication factor?
    a. password
    b. mother's maiden name
    c. city of birth
    d. smart card

53. Which of the following statements about memory cards and smart cards is false?
    a. A memory card is a swipe card that contains user authentication information.
    b. Memory cards are also known as integrated circuit cards (ICCs).
    c. Smart cards contain memory and an embedded chip.
    d. Smart card systems are more reliable than memory card systems.

54. Which biometric method is *most* effective?
    a. iris scan
    b. retina scan
    c. fingerprint
    d. handprint

55. What is a Type I error in a biometric system?
    a. crossover error rate (CER)
    b. false rejection rate (FRR)
    c. false acceptance rate (FAR)
    d. throughput rate

56. Which penetration test provides the testing team with limited knowledge of the network systems and devices using publicly available information, with the organization's security team knowing an attack is coming?
    a. target test
    b. physical test
    c. blind test
    d. double-bind test

57. Which access control type reduces the effect of an attack or other undesirable event?
    a. compensative control
    b. preventive control
    c. detective control
    d. corrective control

58. Which of the following controls is an administrative control?
    a. security policy
    b. CCTV
    c. data backups
    d. locks

59. Which access control model is most often used by routers and firewalls to control access to networks?
    a. discretionary access control
    b. mandatory access control
    c. role-based access control
    d. rule-based access control

60. Which threat is *not* considered a social engineering threat?
    a. phishing
    b. pharming
    c. DoS attack
    d. dumpster diving

61. Which of the following is not used in biometric systems to authenticate individuals?
    a. fingerprinting
    b. keyboard dynamics
    c. iris scan
    d. cognitive password

62. Which of the following is the most important when evaluating different biometric systems?
    a. Type I error
    b. CER
    c. Type II error
    d. the total amount of errors between Type I and Type II

63. Which of the following attacks is most used to uncover passwords?
    a. spoofing
    b. dictionary attack
    c. DoS
    d. WinNuk

64. Which of the following is not a weakness of Kerberos?
    a. The KDC is a single point of failure.
    b. Kerberos is vulnerable to password guessing.
    c. All devices must have Kerberos software to participate.
    d. Kerberos is the de facto standard for distributed networks.

65. Which of the following access control modes uses security labels?
    a. discretionary
    b. nondiscretionary
    c. mandatory
    d. role-based

66. A capability table is bound to which of the following?
    a. subject
    b. object
    c. ACLs
    d. permissions

67. Which of the following is not an example of centralized access control administration technology?
    a. RADIUS
    b. TEMPEST
    c. TACACS
    d. diameter

68. Which of the following best describes the difference between memory and smart cards?
    a. A memory card has a microprocessor and integrated circuits used to process data, whereas a smart card has a magnetic strip that is used to hold information.
    b. A smart card has a microprocessor and integrated circuits used to process data, whereas a memory card has a magnetic strip that is used to hold information.
    c. Memory cards are more tamperproof than smart cards.
    d. Memory cards are cheaper to develop, create, and maintain.

69. Which of the following is a true statement pertaining to intrusion detection systems?
    a. Signature-based systems can detect new attack types.
    b. Signature-based systems cause more false positives than behavior-based systems.
    c. Behavior-based systems maintain a database of patterns to match packets and attacks against them.
    d. Behavior-based systems have a higher number of false positives than signature-based systems.

70. Which of the following is a countermeasure to traffic analysis attacks?
    a. control zones
    b. keystroke monitoring

c. object reuse

d. mandatory access

71. If several subjects access the same media or memory segments, sensitive data may be at risk of being uncovered. This is referred to as:
a. degaussing
b. zeroization
c. object reuse
d. mandatory access

72. Which of the following is not a critical piece in developing a penetration test?
a. Obtain management approval.
b. Conduct war dialing.
c. Establish and outline goals before testing begins.
d. Establish timeline for testing.

| Answer Key: Access Control | |
|---|---|
| 1 | C |
| 2 | C |
| 3 | B |
| 4 | A |
| 5 | B |
| 6 | C |
| 7 | A |
| 8 | B |
| 9 | B |
| 10 | B |
| 11 | B |
| 12 | A |
| 13 | C |
| 14 | A, B |
| 15 | A |
| 16 | A |
| 17 | B, D |
| 18 | C |
| 19 | C |

| 20 | A |
|----|------|
| 21 | A |
| 22 | C |
| 23 | F |
| 24 | D |
| 25 | C |
| 26 | D |
| 27 | B |
| 28 | C |
| 29 | A |
| 30 | A |
| 31 | D |
| 32 | B |
| 33 | B |
| 34 | A |
| 35 | B |
| 36 | A |
| 37 | A, C, D |
| 38 | C |
| 39 | B |
| 40 | B |
| 41 | B |
| 42 | A |
| 43 | B |
| 44 | A |
| 45 | C |
| 46 | B |
| 47 | D |
| 48 | B |
| 49 | C, E |
| 50 | A |
| 51 | C |
| 52 | D |
| 53 | B |
| 54 | A |
| 55 | B |

| | |
|---|---|
| 56 | C |
| 57 | D |
| 58 | A |
| 59 | D |
| 60 | C |
| 61 | D |
| 62 | B |
| 63 | B |
| 64 | D |
| 65 | C |
| 66 | A |
| 67 | B |
| 68 | B |
| 69 | D |
| 70 | D |
| 71 | C |
| 72 | B |

# Cryptography

1. In forensic analysis, taking hashes ensures that the collected evidence retains:
   a. confidentiality
   b. integrity
   c. order of volatility
   d. availability

2. Which of the following security controls provide(s) confidentiality? (Select all that apply)
   a. encryption
   b. certificates
   c. digital signatures
   d. steganography
   e. hashing

3. Steganography allows for:
   a. checking data integrity
   b. calculating hash values
   c. hiding data within another piece of data
   d. data encryption

4. Which of the following security controls provide(s) integrity? (Select all that apply)
   a. hashing
   b. steganography
   c. fault tolerance
   d. digital signatures
   e. nonrepudiation
   f. encryption

5. What is the purpose of nonrepudiation?
   a. to hide one piece of data in another piece of data
   b. to ensure that received data has not changed in transit
   c. to prevent someone from denying that they have taken a specific action
   d. to transform plaintext into ciphertext

6. The two basic techniques for encrypting information include symmetric encryption (also called public key encryption) and asymmetric encryption (also called secret key encryption).
   a. True
   b. False

7. In asymmetric encryption, any message encrypted with the use of the public key can only be decrypted by applying the same algorithm and the matching private key.
   a. True
   b. False

8. The large amount of processing power required to both anergy and decrypt the content of the message causes the symmetric key encryption algorithms

to be much slower as compared to algorithms used in in asymmetric encryption.

a. True

b. False

9. A cryptographic key generated to be used only once within a short time frame is known as a session key.

a. True

b. False

10. In asymmetric encryption, data encrypted with the use of a private key can only be encrypted with the use of a matching policy key.

a. True

b. False

11. The key exchange mechanism whereby the cryptographic key is being delivered over a different channel from the main communication channel (for example, on a USB thumb drive) is an example of an in-band key exchange.

a. True

b. False

12. Block ciphers work by encrypting each plaintext digit one at a time.

a. True

b. False

13. What is the purpose of nonrepudiation?

a. to hide one piece of data in another piece of data

b. to ensure that received data has not changed in transit

c. to prevent someone from denying that they have taken a specific action

d. to transform plaintext into ciphertext

14. Taking hashes ensures that data retains its what?

a. confidentiality

b. integrity

c. order of volatility

d. availability

15. What is the name of a storage solution used to retain copies of private encryption keys?
    a. trusted OS
    b. key escrow
    c. proxy server
    d. recovery agent

16. What is the purpose of steganography?
    a. to check data integrity
    b. to calculate hash values
    c. to hide data within another piece of data
    d. data encryption

17. A digital signature is a hash of a message that uniquely identifies the sender of the message and provides a proof that the message has not changed in transit.
    a. True
    b. False

18. What are the features of elliptic-curve cryptography (ECC)? (Select 2 answers.)
    a. asymmetric encryption
    b. shared key
    c. suitable for small wireless devices
    d. high processing power requirements
    e. symmetric encryption

19. Which of the following answers refers to the applicants/features of quantum cryptography?
    a. high availability
    b. protection against eavesdropping
    c. loop protection
    d. secure key exchange
    e. host-based intrusion detection

20. SHA, MD5, and RIPEMD are examples of:
    a. trust models
    b. encryption algorithms
    c. hash functions
    d. virus signatures

21. Which of the answers listed below refer(s) to the Advanced Encryption Standard (AES)? (Select all that apply)
    a. symmetric-key algorithm
    b. 128-,192-, and 256-bit keys
    c. asymmetric-key algorithm
    d. block cipher algorithm
    e. stream cipher algorithm

22. Unlike stream ciphers, which process data by encrypting individual bits, block ciphers divide data into separate fragments and encrypt each fragment separately.
    a. True
    b. False

23. Which of the following are symmetric-key algorithms? (Select 3 answers.)
    a. AES
    b. DES
    c. RSA
    d. Diffie–Hellman
    e. 3DES

24. Which of the following answers refers to a solution for secure exchange of cryptographic keys? (Select best answer)
    a. Data Encryption Standard (DES)
    b. in-band key exchange
    c. Diffie–Hellman
    d. out-of-band key exchange

25. A computer program (and related protocols) that uses cryptography to provide data security for electronic mail and applications on the internet is known as:
   a. SMTP
   b. PGP
   c. OCSP
   d. OVAL

26. Which of the protocols listed below uses elliptic-curve cryptography for secure exchange of cryptographic keys?
   a. ECC
   b. LANMAN
   c. ECDHE
   d. OCSP

27. Which of the following answers refers to a cryptographic network protocol for secure data communication, remote command-line login, remote command execution, and other secure network services between two networked computers?
   a. telnet
   b. SSH
   c. Bcrypt
   d. TFTP

28. In cryptography, the term *key stretching* refers to a mechanism for extending the length of the cryptographic key to make it more secure against brute-force attacks.
   a. True
   b. False

29. Examples of key stretching algorithms include: (Select 2 answers.)
   a. PBKDF2
   b. RC4
   c. NTLMv2
   d. Bcrypt
   e. FCoE

30. Which of the solutions listed below allow(s) one to check whether a digital certificate has been revoked? (Select all that apply)
   a. CIRT
   b. CRL
   c. OCSP
   d. CRC
   e. ICMP

31. Which of the following provides the faster way for validating a digital certificate?
   a. ICMP
   b. CRL
   c. key escrow
   d. OCSP

32. Copies of lost private encryption keys can be retrieved from a key database by:
   a. power users
   b. recovery agents
   c. end users
   d. backup operators

33. Which of the following terms illustrate(s) the security through obscurity concept? (Select all that apply)
   a. code obfuscation
   b. steganography
   c. SSID broadcast suppression
   d. encryption
   e. substitution ciphers

34. Which of the answers listed below refers to a solution designed to strengthen the security of session keys?
   a. ECB
   b. PFS
   c. EFS
   d. PFX

35. Which of the three states of digital data requires data to be processed in an unencrypted form?
    a. data-in-transit
    b. data-at-rest
    c. data-in-use
    d.

36. In cryptography, the term *secret algorithm* refers to an algorithm designed to be used only for the duration of a single session or transaction.
    a. True
    b. False

37. The term *ephemeral key* refers to an asymmetric key designed to be used only for the duration of a single session or transaction.
    a. True
    b. False

38. What are the characteristic features of a session key? (Select 2 answers.)
    a. used during a single session
    b. asymmetric key
    c. reused during multiple sessions
    d. symmetric key

39. In cryptography, the number of bits in a key used by a cryptographic algorithm is referred to as a key size or key length. The key size determines the maximum number of combinations required to break encryption algorithm; therefore, typically a longer key means stronger cryptographic security.
    a. True
    b. False

40. Unlike stream ciphers, which process data by encrypting individual bits, block ciphers divide data into separate fragments and encrypt each fragment separately.
    a. True
    b. False

41. Which of the following terms is used in conjunction with the assumption that the output of a cryptographic function should be considerably different from the corresponding plaintext input?
    a. confusion
    b. obfuscation
    c. collision
    d. diffusion

42. Which of the terms listed below is used to describe a situation where a small change introduced to the input data before encryption causes large changes in its encrypted version?
    a. diffusion
    b. confusion
    c. obfuscation
    d. collision

43. Digital signatures provide the following: (Select 3 answers.)
    a. integrity
    b. authentication
    c. confidentiality
    d. authorization
    e. nonrepudiation
    f. accounting

44. What are the examples of weak/deprecated cryptographic solutions? (Select 3 answers.)
    a. WEP
    b. AES
    c. SSL
    d. DES
    e. PGP

45. What are the characteristic features of elliptic-curve cryptography (ECC)? (Select 3 answers.)
    a. asymmetric encryption
    b. low processing power requirements
    c. suitable for small wireless services

d. high processing power requirements

e. symmetric encryption

f. not suitable for small wireless services

46. Examples of means that provide randomization during the encryption process include: (Select 3 answers.)

a. cryptographic nonce

b. obfuscation

c. salting

d. initialization vector (IV)

e. shimming

47. Pseudorandom data used in combination with a secret key in WEP and SSL encryption schemes is known as:

a. salt

b. shim

c. IV

d. seed

48. Which of the following answers refers to a type of additional input that increases password complexity and provides better protection against brute-force, dictionary, and rainbow table attacks?

a. seed

b. IV

c. salt

d. shim

49. Pseudorandom data added to a password before hashing is called:

a. shim

b. salt

c. seed

d. IV

50. In asymmetric encryption, any message encrypted with the use of a public key can only be decrypted by applying the same algorithm and a matching private key.
    a. True
    b. False

51. A type of encryption scheme that uses a paired public and private key is known as: (Select 2 answers.)
    a. secret-key encryption
    b. asymmetric encryption
    c. symmetric encryption
    d. public-key encryption
    e. session-key encryption

52. Which of the block cipher modes listed below provides both data integrity and confidentiality?
    a. CBC
    b. GCM
    c. ECB
    d. CTR

53. Which of the following block cipher modes is the simplest/weakest and therefore not recommended for use?
    a. CBC
    b. GCM
    c. ECB
    d. CTR

54. Symmetric encryption algorithms require large amounts of processing power for both encryption and decryption of data, which makes them much slower in comparison to asymmetric encryption ciphers.
    a. True
    b. False

55. A type of encryption scheme where the same key is used to encrypt and decrypt data is referred to as: (Select 3 answers.)
   a. session-key encryption
   b. public-key encryption
   c. symmetric encryption
   d. asymmetric encryption
   e. secret-key encryption

56. Examples of techniques used for encrypting information include symmetric encryption (also called public-key encryption) and asymmetric encryption (also called secret-key encryption, or session-key encryption).
   a. True
   b. False

57. Which of the answers listed below refer to obfuscation methods? (Select 3 answers.)
   a. encryption
   b. steganography
   c. XOR cipher
   d. password salting
   e. ROT13

58. What are the examples of key-stretching algorithms? (Select 2 answers.)
   a. ROT13
   b. Twofish
   c. Bcrypt
   d. DSA
   e. PBKDF2

59. Which of the following are hashing algorithms? (Select all that apply)
   a. MD5
   b. RIPEMD
   c. Bcrypt
   d. HMAC
   e. SHA

60. Which of the algorithms listed below does not fall into the category of asymmetric encryption?
    a. RSA
    b. GPG
    c. DSA
    d. AES
    e. DHE
    f. ECDHE
    g. PGP

61. Which of the following answers refers to a commonly used asymmetric algorithm for secure exchange of symmetric keys?
    a. RC4
    b. Bcrypt
    c. Diffie–Hellman
    d. RIPEMD

62. A cryptographic standard for digital signatures is known as:
    a. DSA
    b. PFS
    c. DES
    d. RSA

63. Which of the algorithms listed below does not belong to the category of asymmetric ciphers?
    a. RC4
    b. DES
    c. RSA
    d. AES
    e. Blowfish
    f. 3DES
    g. Twofish

64. Which of the answers listed below refer to the Advanced Encryption Standard (AES)? (Select 3 answers.)
    a. symmetric-key algorithm
    b. 128-, 192-, and 256-bit keys

c. asymmetric-key algorithm

d. stream cipher algorithm

e. 56-, 112-, and 168-bit keys

f. block cipher algorithm

65. Which of the following cryptographic hash functions is the least vulnerable to attacks?

a. SHA-1

b. RIPEMD

c. SHA-512

d. MD5

66. Which of the cryptographic algorithms listed below is the least vulnerable to attacks?

a. AES

b. DES

c. RC4

d. 3DES

67. Which of the following authentication protocol(s) offer(s) countermeasures against replay attacks? (Select all that apply)

a. IPsec

b. MPLS

c. PAP

d. Kerberos

e. CHAP

68. Which of the following answers lists an example of a cryptographic downgrade attack?

a. MITM

b. KPA

c. POODLE

d. XSRF

69. A situation where the cryptographic hash function produces two different digests for the same data input is referred to as hash collision.
   a. True
   b. False

70. One of the measures for bypassing the failed log-on attempt account lockout policy is to capture any relevant data that might contain the password and brute-force it offline.
   a. True
   b. False

71. An attack against encrypted data that relies heavily on computing power to check all possible keys and passwords until the correct one is found is known as:
   a. replay attack
   b. brute-force attack
   c. dictionary attack
   d. birthday attack

72. Which password attack takes advantage of a predefined list of words?
   a. birthday attack
   b. replay attack
   c. dictionary attack
   d. brute-force attack

73. Rainbow tables are lookup tables used to speed up the process of password guessing.
   a. True
   b. False

74. Which of the following answers refers to the contents of a rainbow table entry?
   a. hash/password
   b. IP address / domain name
   c. username/password
   d. account name / hash

75. Which of the acronyms listed below refers to a cryptographic attack where the attacker has access to both the plaintext and its encrypted version?
    a. KEK
    b. POODLE
    c. KPA
    d. CSRF

76. Which cryptographic attack relies on the concepts of probability theory?
    a. KPA
    b. brute force
    c. dictionary
    d. birthday

77. Which process converts plaintext into ciphertext?
    a. hashing
    b. decryption
    c. encryption
    d. digital signature

78. What occurs when different encryption keys generate the same ciphertext from the same plaintext message?
    a. key clustering
    b. cryptanalysis
    c. key space
    d. confusion

79. Which type of cipher is the Caesar cipher?
    a. polyalphabetic substitution
    b. monoalphabetic substitution
    c. polyalphabetic transposition
    d. monoalphabetic transposition

80. Which encryption system uses a private or secret key that must remain secret between the two parties?
    a. running key cipher
    b. concealment cipher

c. asymmetric algorithm

d. symmetric algorithm

81. What is the most secure encryption scheme?

    a. concealment cipher

    b. symmetric algorithm

    c. onetime pad

    d. asymmetric algorithm

82. Which 3DES implementation encrypts each block of data three times, each time with a different key?

    a. 3DES-EDE3

    b. 3DES-EEE3

    c. 3DES-EDE2

    d. 3DES-EEE2

83. Which of the following is an asymmetric algorithm?

    a. IDEA

    b. Twofish

    c. RC6

    d. RSA

84. Which of the following is *not* a hash function?

    a. ECC

    b. MD6

    c. SHA-2

    d. RIPEMD-160

85. Which PKI component contains a list of all the certificates that have been revoked?

    a. CA

    b. RA

    c. CRL

    d. OCSP

86. Which attack executed against a cryptographic algorithm uses all possible keys until a key is discovered that successfully decrypts the ciphertext?
    a. frequency analysis
    b. reverse engineering
    c. ciphertext-only attack
    d. brute force

87. Which of the following is a set of mathematical rules used in cryptography?
    a. key
    b. algorithm
    c. key space
    d. work factor

88. Which of the following statements is most accurate about the strength of a cryptosystem?
    a. The strength of the cryptosystem comes from the algorithm, secrecy of the key, and length of the key.
    b. The strength of the cryptosystem is determined by its message integrity.
    c. The strength of the cryptosystem relies on whether it's been publicly tested.
    d. Strong cryptosystems have secret algorithms.

89. Which of the following is the method for hiding data in another message or data format so that the very existence of the data is concealed?
    a. substitution
    b. shift alphabet
    c. transposition
    d. steganography

90. Which of the following is a described weakness of the Clipper chip?
    a. It was software-based, and the public wanted hardware implementations.
    b. It was publicly tested, so it was not viewed as a secure mechanism.
    c. Its eighty-bit key was considered too small.
    d. It was based on the Lucifer algorithm.

91. Which of the following is considered a strength of symmetric cryptography?
    a. key distribution
    b. processing speed

c. scalability

d. provides user authenticity as well as confidentiality

92. Which of the following was approved for DES?
    a. Skipjack
    b. Rijndael
    c. Twofish
    d. Lucifer

93. What does ECB stand for?
    a. electronic codebook
    b. encryption control book
    c. encryption codebook
    d. elliptic-curve barometers

94. Which of the following is a framework of programs, data formats, procedures, protocols, and public key cryptography mechanisms working together to enable secure communications?
    a. CA
    b. DSS
    c. PKI
    d. RSA

95. Which of the following best describes a onetime pad?
    a. an encryption scheme that is impossible to break because of its randomness and pad length
    b. an encrypted hash value of a message
    c. a function that takes a variable-length message and turns it on a fixed-length value
    d. a mathematical function that is easier to compute in one direction than in the opposite direction

96. Which of the following is a standard for encryption and digitally signing emails with attachments?
    a. PGP
    b. S/MIME

c. SET

d. SSL

97. Which of the following is used by DES for integrity and authentication purposes?

a. SSL

b. SA

c. ESP

d. MAC

98. Which truly describes the difference between using message authentication code and digital signatures?

a. Digital signatures provide system authentication using symmetric keys.

b. Data origin is provided with private keys in MAC.

c. MAC can only provide system authentication and not user authentication because a private key is not used.

d. Digital signatures use private and symmetric keys to provide data origin and systems and user authentication.

| Cryptography Answer Key | |
| --- | --- |
| 1 | B |
| 2 | A, D |
| 3 | C |
| 4 | A, D, E |
| 5 | C |
| 6 | B |
| 7 | A |
| 8 | B |
| 9 | A |
| 10 | A |
| 11 | B |
| 12 | B |
| 13 | C |
| 14 | B |
| 15 | B |
| 16 | C |
| 17 | A |

| | |
|---|---|
| 18 | A, C |
| 19 | B, D |
| 20 | C |
| 21 | A, B, D |
| 22 | A |
| 23 | A, B, E |
| 24 | C |
| 25 | B |
| 26 | C |
| 27 | B |
| 28 | A |
| 29 | A, D |
| 30 | B, C |
| 31 | D |
| 32 | B |
| 33 | A, B, C, E |
| 34 | B |
| 35 | C |
| 36 | A |
| 37 | A |
| 38 | A, D |
| 39 | A |
| 40 | A |
| 41 | A |
| 42 | A |
| 43 | A, B, E |
| 44 | A, C, D |
| 45 | A, B, C |
| 46 | A, C, D |
| 47 | C |
| 48 | C |
| 49 | B |
| 50 | A |
| 51 | B, C |
| 52 | B |
| 53 | C |

| | |
|---|---|
| 54 | B |
| 55 | A, C, E |
| 56 | B |
| 57 | B, C |
| 58 | C, E |
| 59 | A, B, D, E |
| 60 | D |
| 61 | C |
| 62 | A |
| 63 | C |
| 64 | A, B, F |
| 65 | C |
| 66 | A |
| 67 | A, D, E |
| 68 | C |
| 69 | B |
| 70 | A |
| 71 | B |
| 72 | C |
| 73 | A |
| 74 | A |
| 75 | C |
| 76 | D |
| 77 | C |
| 78 | A |
| 79 | B |
| 80 | D |
| 81 | C |
| 82 | B |
| 83 | D |
| 84 | A |
| 85 | A |
| 86 | D |
| 87 | B |
| 88 | A |
| 89 | D |

| 90 | C |
|----|---|
| 91 | B |
| 92 | D |
| 93 | A |
| 94 | C |
| 95 | A |
| 96 | B |
| 97 | D |
| 99 | C |

## Assets Security

1. As head of sales, Jim is the data owner for the sales department. Which of the following is not Jim's responsibility as data owner?
   a. assigning information classification
   b. dictating how data should be protected
   c. verifying the availability of data
   d. determining how long to retain data

2. Assigning data classification levels can help with all the following except:
   a. the grouping of classified information with hierarchical and restrictive security
   b. ensuring that no sensitive data is not being protected by unnecessary controls
   c. extracting data from a database
   d. lowering the costs of protecting data

3. Susan, an attorney, has been hired to fill a new position at Widgets, Inc.: chief privacy officer (CPO). What is the primary function of her new role?
   a. ensuring the protection of partner data
   b. ensuring the accuracy and protection of company financial information
   c. ensuring that security policies are defined and enforced
   d. ensuring the protection of customer, company, and employee data

4. Jared plays a role in his company's data classification system. In this role, he must practice due care when accessing data and ensure that the data are used only in accordance with allowed policy while abiding by the rules

set for the classification of the data. He does not determine, maintain, or evaluate controls, so what is Jared's role?

   a. data owner

   b. data custodian

   c. data user

   d. information systems auditor

5. Michael is charged with developing a data classification program for his company. Which of the following should he do first?

   a. understand the different levels of protection that must be provided

   b. specify data classification criteria

   c. identify the data custodian

   d. determine protection mechanisms for each classification level

6. Which of the following is *not* a factor in determining the sensitivity of data?

   a. who should be accessing the data

   b. the value of the data

   c. how the data will be used

   d. the level of damage that could be caused should the data be exposed

7. What is the chief security responsibility of a data owner?

   a. determine how the data should be preserved

   b. determine the data classification

   c. determine the data value

   d. determine how the data will be used

8. Which is the most valuable technique when determining if a specific security control should be implemented?

   a. risk analysis

   b. cost–benefit analysis

   c. ALE results

   d. identifying the vulnerabilities and threats causing the risk

9. Which of the following is the *least* important stage in the life-cycle management of information?

   a. data specification and classification

   b. continuous monitoring and auditing of data access

c. data archival

d. database immigration

10. The requirement of erasure is the end of the media life cycle if the media contains sensitive information. Which of the following best describes purging?

    a. Hanging the polarization of the atoms in the media.

    b. It is unacceptable when media are to be reused in the same physical environment for the same purposes.

    c. Data formerly on the media is made unrecoverable by overwriting it with a pattern.

    d. Information is mode unrecoverable, even with extraordinary effort.

11. Sam plans to establish mobile phone service using the personal information he has stolen from his former boss. What type of identity theft is this?

    a. phishing

    b. true name

    c. pharming

    d. account takeover

12. Which of the following are common military categories of data classification?

    a. top secret, secret, classified, unclassified

    b. top secret, secret, confidential, private

    c. top secret, secret, confidential, unclassified

    d. classified, unclassified, public

13. Joan needs to document a data classification scheme for her organization. Which criteria should she use to guide her decision?

    a. the value of the data and the age of the data

    b. legal responsibilities based on ISO regulations

    c. who will be responsible for protecting the data and how

    d. how an adverse data breach would be handled

14. Which of the following means of data removal makes data unrecoverable even with extraordinary effort, such as with physical forensics in a laboratory?
    a. deletion of the data
    b. sanitization of the media
    c. purging via overwriting
    d. none of these

**Assets Security Answer Key**

| 1 | C |
|----|----|
| 2 | C |
| 3 | D |
| 4 | C |
| 5 | A |
| 6 | C |
| 7 | B |
| 8 | B |
| 9 | D |
| 10 | D |
| 11 | B |
| 12 | C |
| 13 | A |
| 14 | C |

# Physical Security

1. Which of the following is an example of preventing an internal threat?
    a. a door lock system on the server room
    b. an electric fence surrounding the facility
    c. armed guards outside the facility
    d. parking lot cameras

2. Which of the following is not an example of a natural threat?
    a. flood
    b. bombing
    c. earthquake
    d. tornado

3. Which of the following is a system threat?
   a. loss of utilities
   b. bombing
   c. earthquake
   d. tornado

4. What is the recommended optimal relative humidity range for computer operations?
   a. 10%–30%
   b. 20%–40%
   c. 30%–50%
   d. 40%–60%

5. What is the most prevalent cause of computer center fires?
   a. human error
   b. electrical distribution systems
   c. lighting systems
   d. arson

6. Which of the following is not an example of a man-made threat?
   a. bombing
   b. arson
   c. flood
   d. collusion

7. Which of the following extinguishers is designed to address electrical equipment fires?
   a. class A
   b. class B
   c. class C
   d. class D

8. Class K extinguishers are designed to address what type of fire?
   a. that from cooking oil or fat
   b. that from flammable liquids
   c. that from combustible metals
   d. that from ordinary combustibles

9. Which of the following is not a politically motivated threat?
   a. power outage
   b. bombing
   c. strike
   d. civil disobedience

10. Which of the following is not one of the threat main strategies that guide CPTED?
   a. Natural Access Control
   b. Natural Surveillance Reinforcement
   c. Natural Territorials Reinforcement
   d. Natural Surveillance

| Physical Security Answer Key | |
|---|---|
| 1 | A |
| 2 | B |
| 3 | A |
| 4 | D |
| 5 | B |
| 6 | B |
| 7 | C |
| 8 | A |
| 9 | A |
| 10 | B |

**Telecommunications and Network Security**

1. At which layer of the IOS model does the encapsulation process begin?
   a. transport
   b. application
   c. physical
   d. session

2. Which two layers of the OSI model are represented by the link layer of the TCP/IP model? (Choose two)
   a. data link
   b. physical
   c. session
   d. application
   e. presentation

3. Which of the following represents the range of port numbers that are referred to as "well-known" port numbers?
   a. 49152–65535
   b. 0–1023
   c. 1024–49151
   d. all above 500

4. What is the port number for http?
   a. 23
   b. 443
   c. 80
   d. 110

5. What protocol in the TCP/IP suite resolves IP addresses to MAC addresses?
   a. ARP
   b. TCP
   c. IP
   d. ICMP

6. How many bits are contained in an IPv4 IP address?
   a. 128
   b. 48
   c. 32
   d. 64

7. Which of the following is a class C address?
   a. 172.16.5.6
   b. 192.168.5.54
   c. 10.6.5.8
   d. 224.6.6.6

8. Which of the following is a private IP address?
   a. 10.2.6.6
   b. 172.15.6.6
   c. 191.6.6.6
   d. 223.54.5.5

9. Which service converts private IP addresses to public IP addresses?
   a. DHCP
   b. DNS
   c. NAT
   d. WEP

10. Which type of transmission uses stop and start bits?
   a. asynchronous
   b. unicast
   c. multicast
   d. synchronous

| Telecommunications and Network Security Answer Key | |
|---|---|
| 1 | B |
| 2 | A, B |
| 3 | B |
| 4 | C |
| 5 | A |
| 6 | C |
| 7 | B |
| 8 | A |
| 9 | C |
| 10 | A |

# Legal, Regulations, Investigations, and Compliance

1. Which type of crime occurs when a computer is used as a tool to help commit a crime?
   a. computer-assisted crime
   b. incidental computer crime
   c. computer-targeted crime
   d. computer prevalence crime

2. Which type of law system is based on written laws and does not use precedence?
   a. common law
   b. civil code law
   c. criminal law
   d. customary law

3. Which of the following protects intellectual property such as symbol, sound, or expression that identifies a product or an organization from being used by another organization?
   a. patent
   b. copyright
   c. trademark
   d. trade secret

4. What is another name for the Public Company Accounting Reform and Investor Protection Act of 2002?
   a. Kennedy–Kassebaum Act
   b. USA PATRIOT
   c. Obamacare
   d. Sarbanes–Oxley Act

5. Which term is the status of being legally responsible to another entity because of your actions or negligence?
   a. liability
   b. due care
   c. due diligence
   d. negligence

6. What is the first step of the incident-response process?
   a. Respond to the incident.
   b. Detect the incident.
   c. Report the incident.
   d. Recover from the incident.

7. What is the second step of the forensic investigations process?
   a. identification
   b. collection
   c. preservation
   d. examination

8. Which of the following is *not* one of the five rules of evidence?
   a. Be accurate.
   b. Be complete.
   c. Be admissible.
   d. Be volatile.

9. Which type of evidence has been reproduced from an original or substituted for an original item?
   a. secondary evidence
   b. best evidence
   c. hearsay evidence
   d. direct evidence

10. Which of the following is *not* one of the four mandatory canons of the (ISC)² Code of Ethics?
    a. Provide diligent and competent service to principals.
    b. Always use a computer in ways that ensure consideration and respect of other people and their property.
    c. Advance and protect the profession.
    d. Act honorably, honestly, justly, responsibly, and legally.

| Legal, Regulations, Investigations, and Compliance Answer Key | |
|:---:|:---:|
| 1 | A |
| 2 | B |
| 3 | C |
| 4 | D |
| 5 | A |
| 6 | B |
| 7 | C |
| 8 | D |
| 9 | A |
| 10 | B |

# Software Development Security

1. Which of the following is the last step in the system development life cycle?
   a. operate/maintain
   b. dispose
   c. acquire/develop
   d. initiate

2. In which of the following stages of the software development life cycle is the software coded?
   a. gather requirements
   b. design
   c. develop
   d. test/validate

3. Which of the following initiatives was developed by the Department of Homeland Security?
   a. WASC
   b. BSI

c. OWASP

d. ISO

4. Which of the following development models provides no formal control mechanisms to provide feedback?

a. waterfall

b. V-shaped

c. build and fix

d. spiral

5. Which language type delivers instructions directly to the processor?

a. assembly language

b. high-level language

c. machine language

d. natural language

6. Which term describes how many different tasks a module can carry out?

a. polymorphism

b. cohesion

c. coupling

d. data structures

7. Which term describes a standard for communication between processes on the same computer?

a. CORBA

b. DCOM

c. COM

d. SOA

8. Which of the following is a Microsoft technology?

a. ActiveX

b. Java

c. SOA

d. CORBA

9. Which of the following is the number or rows in a relation?
   a. tuple
   b. schema
   c. cardinality
   d. degree

10. In which database model can an object have multiple parents?
    a. hierarchical
    b. object-oriented
    c. network
    d. object-relational

| Software Development Security Answer Key | |
|---|---|
| 1 | B |
| 2 | C |
| 3 | B |
| 4 | C |
| 5 | C |
| 6 | B |
| 7 | C |
| 8 | A |
| 9 | C |
| 10 | C |

# Security Architecture and Design

1. Which of the following is provided if the data cannot be read?
   a. integrity
   b. confidentiality
   c. availability
   d. defense-in-depth

2. Which of the following ISO/IEC 42010:2011 terms is the set of documents that convey the architecture in a formal manner?
   a. architecture

b. stakeholder

c. architectural description (AD)

d. view

3. In a distributed environment, which of the following is software that ties the client and server software together?

a. embedded systems

b. mobile code

c. virtual computing

d. middleware

4. Which of the following is a relatively small amount of very high-speed RAM that holds the instructions and data from primary method?

a. cache

b. firmware

c. flash memory

d. FPGA

5. In which CPU mode are the processors or cores handed work on a round-robin basis, thread by thread?

a. cache mode

b. symmetric mode

c. asymmetric mode

d. overlap mode

6. Which of the following compromises the components (hardware, firmware, and/or software) that are trusted to enforce the security policy of the system?

a. security perimeter

b. reference monitor

c. trusted computer base (TCB)

d. security kernel

7. Which of the following is the dividing line between the trusted parts of the system and those that are untrusted?

a. security perimeter

b. reference monitor

c. trusted computer base (TCB)

d. security kernel

8. Which of the following is a system component that enforces access controls on an object?

    a. security perimeter

    b. reference monitor

    c. trusted computer base (TCB)

    d. security kernel

9. Which of the following is the hardware, firmware, and software elements of a TCB that implements the reference monitor concept?

    a. security perimeter

    b. reference monitor

    c. trusted computer base (TCB)

    d. security kernel

10. Which of the following frameworks is a two-dimensional model that intersects communication interrogatives (what, why, where, and so on) with various viewpoints (planner, owner, designer, and so on)?

    a. SABSA

    b. Zachman framework

    c. TOGAF

    d. ITIL

| Security Architecture and Design Answer Key ||
|---|---|
| 1 | B |
| 2 | C |
| 3 | D |
| 4 | A |
| 5 | B |
| 6 | C |
| 7 | A |
| 8 | B |
| 9 | D |
| 10 | B |

# Operations Security

1. Which of the following refers to allowing users access only to resources required to do their jobs?
   a. job rotation
   b. separation of duties
   c. need-to-know / least privilege
   d. mandatory vacation

2. Which of the following is an example of an intangible asset?
   a. disk drive
   b. recipes
   c. people
   d. server

3. Which of the following is not a guideline for securing hardware?
   a. Change all default administrator passwords on the devices.
   b. Use telnet rather than SSH.
   c. Limit physical access to these devices.
   d. Manage critical system locally.

4. Which of the following is also called disk striping?
   a. RAID 0
   b. RAID 1
   c. RAID 2
   d. RAID 5

5. Which of the following is also called disk mirroring?
   a. RAID 0
   b. RAID 1
   c. RAID 2
   d. RAID 5

6. Which of the following is comprised of high-capacity storage devices that are connected by a high-speed private (separate from the LAN) network using storage-specific switches?
   a. HSM
   b. SAN
   c. NAS
   d. RAID

7. Which of the following uses a method such as degaussing to make the old data unavailable even with forensics?
   a. data clearing
   b. data purging
   c. remanence
   d. data duplication

8. A backup power supply is an example of:
   a. SLAs
   b. MTBR
   c. redundancy
   d. cardinality

9. Which of the following describes the average amount of time it will take to get the device fixed and back online?
   a. MTBF
   b. MTTR
   c. HSM
   d. SLA

10. Which of the following is not a step in incident response management?
    a. detect
    b. respond
    c. monitor
    d. report

| Operations Security Answer Key | |
|:---:|:---:|
| 1 | C |
| 2 | B |
| 3 | B |
| 4 | A |
| 5 | B |
| 6 | B |
| 7 | B |
| 8 | C |
| 9 | B |
| 10 | C |

# Disaster Recovery

1. What is a catastrophe?
   a. A temporary interruption that occurs due to malfunction or failure.
   b. A suddenly occurring event that has a long-term negative impact in life.
   c. A disaster that has a much wider and much longer impact than other disasters.
   d. A disaster that occurs when a device fails.

2. What is the first step in a business impact analysis (BIA)?
   a. Identify recovery priorities.
   b. Identify outage impacts and estimate downtime.
   c. Identify resource requirements.
   d. Identify critical processes and resources.

3. What is recovery time objective?
   a. The shortest period after a disaster or disruptive event within which a resource or function must be restored if one wishes to avoid unacceptable consequences.
   b. The point in time to which the disrupted resource or function must be returned.

c. The maximum amount of time that an organization can tolerate a single resource or function being down.

d. The average time required to repair a single resource or function when a disaster or disruption occurs.

4. Which term is used for a leased facility that contains all the resources needed for full operation?
   a. cold site
   b. hot site
   c. warm site
   d. tertiary site

5. Which of the following is *not* a backup type?
   a. full
   b. incremental
   c. grandfather/father/son
   d. tertiary site

6. Which electronic backup type stores data on optical disks and uses robotics to load and unload the optical disks as needed?
   a. optical jukebox
   b. hierarchical storage management
   c. tape vaulting
   d. replication

7. What is fail soft?
   a. The capacity of a system to switch over to a backup system if a failure in the primary system occurs.
   b. The capability of a system to terminate noncritical processes when a failure occurs.
   c. A software product that provides load-balancing services.
   d. High-capacity storage devices that are connected by a high-speed private network using storage-specific switches.

8. Which team is *not* defined as part of the business continuity plan (BCP)?
   a. media relations team
   b. security team

c. recovery team

d. human resources team

9. Which test is the most cost-effective and efficient way to identify areas of overlap in the plan before conducting higher-level testing?

   a. tabletop exercise

   b. checklist test

   c. parallel test

   d. simulation test

10. Which is the first step in business community planning according to NIST SP 800-34 R1?

    a. Conduct business impact analysis (BIA).

    b. Develop contingency planning policy.

    c. Identify preventive controls.

    d. Create recovery strategies.

| Disaster Recovery Answer Key | |
|---|---|
| 1 | C |
| 2 | D |
| 3 | A |
| 4 | B |
| 5 | C |
| 6 | A |
| 7 | B |
| 8 | D |
| 9 | A |
| 10 | B |

**Information Security Governance and Risk Management**

1. What is vulnerability?

   a. the entity that carries out a threat

   b. when an organizational asset is exposed to losses

   c. an absence or weakness of a countermeasure that is in place

   d. a control that reduces risk

2. Which ISO/IEC standard gives an overview and vocabulary of information security management?
   a. ISO/IEC 27000
   b. ISO/IEC 27001
   c. ISO/IEC 27002
   d. ISO/IEC 27003

3. Which framework uses the six communication questions (What, Where, When, Why, Who, and How) and intersects with six layers (operational, component, physical, logical, conceptual, and contextual)?
   a. Six Sigma
   b. SABSA
   c. ITIL
   d. ISO/IEC 27000 series

4. What is the first stage of the security program life cycle?
   a. Plan and organize.
   b. Implement.
   c. Operate and maintain.
   d. Monitor and evaluate.

5. Which group of threat agents includes hardware and software failure, malicious code, and new technologies?
   a. human
   b. natural
   c. environmental
   d. technical

6. Which term indicates the monetary impact of each threat occurrence?
   a. ARO
   b. ALE
   c. EF
   d. SLE

7. What is risk avoidance?
   a. Risk that is left over after safeguards have been implemented.
   b. Terminating the activity that causes a risk, or choosing an alternative that is not as risky.

c. Passing a risk to a third party.

d. Defining the acceptable risk level the organization can tolerate and reducing the risk to that level.

8. Which security polices provide instruction on acceptable and unacceptable activities?

a. informative security policies

b. regulatory security policies

c. system-specific security policies

d. advisory security policies

9. What is the highest military security level?

a. confidential

b. top secret

c. private

d. sensitive

10. Which organization role determines the classification level of the information to protect the data for which the person in such a role is responsible?

a. data owner

b. data custodian

c. security administrator

d. security analyst

**Information Security Governance and Risk Management Answer Key**

| 1 | C |
|---|---|
| 2 | A |
| 3 | B |
| 4 | A |
| 5 | D |
| 6 | D |
| 7 | B |
| 8 | D |
| 9 | B |
| 10 | A |

# Secure Network Protocols

1. Which of the answers listed below refers to a deprecated TLS-based method for securing SMTP?
   a. PPTP
   b. STARTTLS
   c. L2TP
   d. SMTPS

2. Which of the following answers refers to a secure implementation of a protocol used for synchronizing clocks over a computer network?
   a. NTPsec
   b. SNMP
   c. SRTP
   d. IPsec

3. What are the characteristic features of the secure version of IMAP? (Select all that apply)
   a. TCP port 143
   b. Secure Sockets Layer (SSL)M
   c. TCP port 993
   d. Transport Layer Security (TLS)
   e. TCP port 995

4. Which of the answers listed below refer(s) to POP3S encrypted communication? (Select all that apply)
   a. TCP port 993
   b. Secure Sockets Layer (SSL)
   c. TCP port 995
   d. Transport Layer Security (TLS)
   e. TCP port 110

5. Which of the following protocols are used for securing http connections? (Select 2 answers.)
   a. SCP
   b. EFS
   c. SSL

d. TLS

e. STP

6. A secure version of the http protocol offering traffic encryption is known as: (Select all that apply)

a. HSPA

b. http over SSL

c. HSRP

d. http over TLS

e. https

7. Which version(s) of the SNMP protocol offer(s) authentication based on community strings sent in an unencrypted form? (Select all that apply)

a. SNMPv1

b. SNMPv2

c. SNMPv3

d. SNMPv4

8. Of the three existing versions of the Simple Network Management Protocol (SNMP), versions 1 and 2 (9SNMPv1 and SNMPv2) offer authentication based on community strings sent in an unencrypted form (in cleartext). SNMPv3 provides packet encryption, authentication, and hashing mechanisms that allow for checking whether data has changed in transit (i.e., data integrity).

a. True

b. False

9. FTPS is an extension to the Secure Shell (SSH) protocol and runs by default on port number 22.

a. True

b. False

10. A network protocol for secure file transfer over Secure Shell (SSH) is called:

a. TFTP

b. SFTP

c. telnet

d. FTPS

11. Secure File Transfer Protocol (SFTP) is an extension to the FTP that adds support for the Transport Layer Security (TLS) and the Secure Sockets Layer (SSL) cryptographic protocols.
    a. True
    b. False

12. Which of the following protocols allow(s) for secure file transfer? (Select all that apply)
    a. FTPS
    b. TFTP
    c. FTP
    d. SFTP
    e. SCP

13. LDAPS is an example of:
    a. authentication protocol
    b. secure directory access protocol
    c. address resolution protocol
    d. file exchange protocol

14. Which protocol enables secure, real-time delivery of audio and video over an IP network?
    a. S/MIME
    b. RTP
    c. SIP
    d. SRTP

15. Multipurpose internet mail extension (MIME) specification extends the mail message format beyond simple text, enabling the transfer of graphics, audio, and video files over the internet mail system. Secure MIME (S/MIME) is an enhanced version of the MIME protocol that enables email security features by providing encryption, authentication, message integrity, and other related services.
    a. True
    b. False

16. Which of the protocols listed below was designed as a secure replacement for telnet?
    a. CHAP
    b. FTP
    c. SNMP
    d. SSH

17. Which of the following answers refers to a cryptographic protocol for secure data communication, remote command-line login, remote command execution, and other secure network services?
    a. telnet
    b. SSH
    c. Bcrypt
    d. TFTP

18. A suite of security extensions for an internet service that translates domain names into IP addresses is known as:
    a. EDNS
    b. DNSSEC
    c. split DNS
    d. DDNS

## Wireless Security

1. Which of the answers listed below refers to a solution allowing administrators to block internet access for users until they perform required action?
   a. honeypot
   b. quarantine network
   c. captive portal
   d. firewall

2. Wi-Fi Protected Setup (WPS) is a network security standard that simplifies configuration of a new wireless network by providing nontechnical users with the capability to easily configure network security settings and add new devices to an existing network. WPS has known vulnerabilities, and

disabling this functionality is one recommended way of securing wireless networks.
   a. True
   b. False

3. What are the characteristic features of WPA/WPA2 Enterprise mode? (Select 2 answers.)
   a. suitable for large corporate networks
   b. does not require an authentication server
   c. suitable for all types of wireless LANs
   d. requires RADIUS authentication server

4. Which of the following would be the best solution for securing a small network or an authentication server?
   a. WPA-PSK
   b. WPA2 Enterprise
   c. WPA2-PSK
   d. WPA Enterprise

5. Extensible Authentication Protocol (EAP) is an authentication framework frequently used in wireless networks and point-to-point connections. EAP provides an authentication framework, not a specific authentication mechanism. There are many authentication mechanisms (referred to as EAP methods) that can be used with EAP. Wireless networks take advantage of several EAP methods, including PEAP, EAP-FAST, EAP-TLS, and EAP-TTLS.
   a. True
   b. False

6. Which of the following EAP methods listed below relies on client-side and server-side certificates to perform authentication?
   a. EAP-TLS
   b. PEAP
   c. EAP-TTLS
   d. EAP-FAST

7. Which of the following EAP methods offers the highest level of security?
   a. PEAP
   b. EAP-FAST
   c. EAP-TLS
   d. EAP-TTLS

8. A security protocol designed to strengthen existing WEB implementations without requiring the replacement of legacy hardware is known as:
   a. PEAP
   b. TKIP
   c. CCMP
   d. WPA2

9. AES-based encryption mode implemented in WPA2 is known as:
   a. CCMP
   b. ECB
   c. CBC
   d. TKIP

10. Wired Equivalent Privacy (WEP) and Wi-Fi Protected Access (WPA) are encryption standards designed for security wireless networks. WEP is an older standard and, because of its vulnerabilities, is not recommended. WPA was designed as an interim replacement for WEP, and WPA2 was introduced as the official standard offering the strongest security of the three.
    a. True
    b. False

11. A wireless disassociation attack is a type of:
    a. downgrade attack
    b. brute-force attack
    c. denial-of-service (Dos) attack
    d. cryptographic attack

12. What is the name of a technology used for contactless payment transactions?
    a. NCF
    b. SDN

c. PED

d. WAP

13. Which of the following wireless technologies enables identification and tracking of tags attached to objects?

a. WTLS

b. GPS

c. RFID

d. WAF

14. Gaining unauthorized access to a Bluetooth device is referred to as:

a. phishing

b. Bluejacking

c. tailgating

d. Bluesnarfing

15. The practice of sending unsolicited messages over Bluetooth is called:

a. SPIM

b. Bluejacking

c. vishing

d. Bluesnarfing

16. Which of the wireless technologies listed below are deprecated and should not be used because of their known vulnerabilities? (Select 2 answers.)

a. WPS

b. WAP

c. WPA2

d. WAF

e. WEP

17. A wireless jamming attack is a type of what?

a. cryptographic attack

b. denial-of-service (Dos) attack

c. brute-force attack

d. downgrade attack

18. The term *evil twin* refers to a rogue wireless access point (WAP) set up for eavesdropping or stealing sensitive user data. Evil twin replaces the legitimate access point by advertising its own presence with the same service set identifier (SSID, a.k.a. network name) and appears as a legitimate access point to connecting host.
    a. True
    b. False

19. A type of wireless attack designed to exploit vulnerabilities of WEP is known as:
    a. MITM attack
    b. Smurf attack
    c. IV attack
    d. Xmas attack

20. Which of the following security protocols is the least susceptible to wireless replay attacks?
    a. WPA2-CCMP
    b. WPA-TKIP
    c. WPA2-PSK
    d. WPA-CCMP
    e. WPA2-TKIP

## Wireless Security Answer Key

| 1  | D       |
|----|---------|
| 2  | A       |
| 3  | B, C, D |
| 4  | B, C, D |
| 5  | C, D    |
| 6  | B, D, E |
| 7  | A, B    |
| 8  | A       |
| 9  | B       |
| 10 | B       |
| 11 | B       |

| 12 | A, D, E |
|---|---|
| 13 | B |
| 14 | D |
| 15 | A |
| 16 | D |
| 17 | B |
| 18 | B |
| 19 | C |
| 20 | A |
| 21 | A, D |
| 22 | C |
| 23 | A |
| 24 | A |
| 25 | C |
| 26 | B |
| 27 | A |
| 28 | A |
| 29 | C |
| 30 | A |
| 31 | C |
| 32 | D |
| 33 | B |
| 34 | A, E |
| 35 | B |
| 36 | A |
| 37 | C |
| 38 | A |

# About the Author

## 1. Preamble

Joseph O. Esin is a professor of computer information systems/cybersecurity, a Fellow at the Washington Center for Cybersecurity Research and Development (FWCCRD), and a Fellow at the Botanical Research Institute of Texas (FBRIT). Esin has twenty-nine years of experience in educational research and publishing; thirty years of academic instruction in computer information systems, networking technologies, management information systems, information security, defensive security, physical security, and principles of networking cybersecurity at undergraduate, graduate and post-graduate levels; ten years of experience in higher education accreditation processes in accordance with the guidelines set forth by Southern Association of Colleges and Schools (SACS) Commission on Colleges; five years of experience in accreditation processes in accordance with the standards set forth by the Accreditation Council for Business Schools and Programs (ACBSP); fifteen years of experience in supervising of doctoral dissertations, masters theses and undergraduate senior class projects; fifteen years of experience in academic and administrative computing; ten years of experience as a publishing editor of the *Journal of Educational Research and Technology* (JERT); and five years of experience in grant writing via the National Science Foundation (NSF). Elected by his peers at Jarvis Christian College to serve as the vice chairman of faculty senate for 2017-2018 academic year, he was re-elected for the 2018 and 2019 academic years, serving three consecutive terms.

## 2. Education

Professor Esin holds a Bachelor of Science degree in biology from Saint Louis University, St. Louis, Missouri; a Master of Arts in theology from the

Society of Jesus College of Divinity, St. Louis, Missouri; and a doctorate in computer education and information systems from the United States International University, San Diego, California. The state of California awarded him a Lifetime Collegiate Instructor's Credential in 1989, and in 1996, the United States Department of Justice approved and conferred on him the honor of Outstanding Professor of Research in recognition of his contributions to academic excellence. He met the selection criteria for inclusion in the 1992–93, 1994–95, 1996–97, and 2015–16 editions of *Who's Who in American Education* for demonstration of achievement and outstanding academic leadership in computer information technology, thereby contributing significantly to the betterment of contemporary society.

Furthermore, he met the selection criteria for inclusion in the 1993–94 edition of the *Directory of International Biography*, Cambridge, England, for demonstration of achievement and outstanding academic leadership in computer information technology, thereby contributing significantly to the betterment of contemporary society. He served as a member of doctoral dissertation committees at Southern Methodist University, Dallas, Texas (1998–2000); Jackson State University, Jackson, Mississippi (2010–2011); and University of Calabar, Nigeria (2014–present). He is a fellow at the Botanical Research Institute of Texas (FBRIT).

## 3. Professional Background

From 1988 to 2000, Joseph O. Esin was a professor of computer information technology, and from 1991 to 2000, he was a director of higher education accreditation operations in accordance with the guidelines set forth by the SACS Commission on Colleges. He served as associate dean of academic affairs and deputy provost at Paul Quinn College, Dallas, Texas, from 1997 to 2000. He is currently a professor of computer information systems and cybersecurity at Jarvis Christian College, Hawkins, Texas. He served as a visiting professor of research at the University at Calabar, 2013–19; visiting professor of cybersecurity at Thomas Edition State University, New Jersey; and visiting professor of cybersecurity at University of the Cumberlands, Kentucky; and was appointed a tenured professor by the computer science department at the University of Calabar.

## 4. Book Publications

Professor Esin is the author of six books, as follows:

- *The Power of Endurance*. Bloomington, IN: iUniverse, 2008. ISBN: 978-595-48299-3.
- *The Evolution of Instructional Technology*. Bloomington, IN: iUniverse, 2011. ISBN: 978-4620-3212-9.
- *The Messianic View of the Kingdom of God*. Bloomington, IN: iUniverse, 2011. ISBN: 978-4620-2083-6.
- *Global Education Reform*. Bloomington, IN: iUniverse, 2013. ISBN: 978-4759-7102-6.
- *System Overview of Cyber-Technology in a Digitally Connected Society*. Bloomington, IN: AuthorHouse, 2017. ISBN: 978-1-5246-5706-2.
- *Landscape of Cybersecurity Threats and Forensic Inquiry*. Bloomington, IN: AuthorHouse, 2017. ISBN: 978-1-5462-1705-3.
- *Ready for Publication: Equity of Cybersecurity in the Education System— from High School through Post-Graduate Studies*.

## 5. Professional Research Publications

Professor Esin is the author of several professional journal articles, as follows:

- "High Level of Teacher's Apprehension (HLTA) about the Use of Computers in the Educational Process" (1991). https//www.jemls.com.
- "Computer Literacy for Teachers: The Role of Computer Technology in the Educational Process" (1992). https//www.jemls.com.
- "Strategies of Developing and Implementing Academic Computing in Colleges and Universities" (1992). https//www.jemls.com.
- "Faculty Development: Effective Use of Applications Software in the Classroom for Instruction" (1993). https//www.jemls.com.
- "Strategic Planning for Computer Integration in Higher Education through the Year 2000" (1994). https//www.jemls.com.
- "The Challenge of Networking Technologies" (1995). https//www.jemls.com.
- "The Design and Use of Instructional Technology in Schools, Colleges, and Universities" (1997). https//www.jemls.com.

- "Decay of Nigerian Educational System" (2013). https//www.thejert.com/issues.
- "Emerging Impact of Information Technology in Education and Community" (2013). https//www.thejert.com/issues.
- "Balanced Salary Structure for Academic Professors and Allied Educators as a Pathway to Quality Education" (2014). https//www.thejert.com/issues.
- "The Discovery of Computer Information Technology Is an Avenue for Educational Transformation in a Changing Society of Today and Tomorrow." https//www.jert.com/issues.
- "Integration of Technology in Education, Instruction, and Learning in a Connected Society" (2015). https//www.thejert.com/issues.
- "Overview of Cyber Security: Endangerment of Cybercrime on Vulnerable Innocent Global Citizens" (2016). https//www.thejert.com/issues.
- "From Analog to Digital: Overcoming Widespread Implementation of Wireless Information Technology on a Vulnerable Global Society" (2016). https//www.thejert.com/issues.
- "Cybersecurity Professional Education and Inquiry" (2017). https://www.washingtoncybercenter.com/publications-projects.
- "Imminent Cybersecurity Threats and Vulnerability of Organizations and Educational System" (2017). https://www.washingtoncybercenter.com/publications-projects.
- "Escalating Outcome of Cyber-Attacks on Healthcare Organizations" (2017). https://www.washingtoncybercenter.com/publications-projects.
- "From Historic to Present Day Culture of Social Engineering Attack" (2018). https://www.washingtoncybercenter.com/publications-projects.
- "Eliminating Gender Disparity in Cybersecurity Professions through Education" (2018). https://www.washingtoncybercenter.com/publications-projects.
- "Offensive and Defensive Approach to Ethical Hacking" (2018). https://www.washingtoncybercenter.com/publications-projects.
- "Imminent Threats of Cloud Computing Technology in Healthcare Operation" (2019). https//www.thejert.com/issues.
- "A Call for Concern: The Unbalanced Representation of Minorities and Women in Cybersecurity Profession" (2019). https://www.washingtoncybercenter.com/publications-projects.

- "Appeal for Equilibrium: Unbalanced Culture of Women and Minorities in Cybersecurity Domain" (2020): 35–45. www.tesu.edu/ast/women-and-minorities-in-technology/journal.
- "Amalgamation of Cryptography and Stenography on Global Society Systems" (2020). https//www.thejert.com/issues.
- "Time ahead of 2020 COVID-19 Pandemic: Outgrowth of Cloud Encryption Algorithm on Biometric Authentication Analysis" (2020). https://www.washingtoncybercenter.com/publications-projects, blog—June 2020.
- "Protagonist of Digital Biometric Authentication and Forensic Analysis" (2020): 35–45. https://www.washingtoncybercenter.com/publications-projects.
- "Impulsive Time ahead of Healthcare Operation in Event of the Next Global COVID-19 Pandemic" (2020): 35–45. https://www.washingtoncybercenter.com/publications-projects.
- "Unbalanced Tradition ahead of Higher Education System in Event of the Next COVID-19 Pandemic" (2020): 35–45. https//www.thejert.com/issues.
- Future Pathway: Overcoming the Sustained Challenges in Digital Forensic Investigation Process (2021). https://www.washingtoncybercenter.com/publications-projects.

## 6. Professional Certifications

1. Network+ certifications
2. Certified Apple educator
3. Microsoft Certified Trainer (MCT)
4. Certified Novell Administrator (CNA)
5. CompTIA A+ (hardware and software)
6. Micro Certification Subnetting (MCS)
7. Access Data Certified Examiner (ADCE)
8. Cisco Certified Network Associate (CCNA)
9. Microsoft Certified Systems Engineer (MCSE)
10. Microsoft Certified Systems Administrator (MCSA)

11. Microsoft Certified Database Administrator (MCDBA)
12. Micro Certification Fundamental Cryptography (MCFC)
13. Micro Certification Privileged Password Security (MCPPS)
14. Micro Certification Organizational Data Security Fundamentals (MCOSF)

———⊗⊗⊗———

Professor Esin is guided by the philosophy that to achieve
what is possible, you must attempt the impossible.